You Shall Be

Baptized

in the Holy Spirit

Acts 1:5

Know the Power of the Holy Spirit

Elsie Fuhrman

Eldo Publishers
2074 Pleasantview Drive
New Brighton, MN 55112

You Shall Be Baptized in the Holy Spirit
Acts 1:5

Eldo Publishers
2074 Pleasantview Drive
New Brighton, MN 55112

ISBN 0-9672203-0-0

Printed in the USA by

MORRIS PUBLISHING

3212 East Highway 30 • Kearney, NE 68847 • 1-800-650-7888

Acknowledgments

I want to give special thanks to Burnadeen Soderlind for her continuous encouragement to me while writing this manuscript and for her editing assistance. Her critique and input contributed greatly to this book. To Joy McComb, I offer my thanks and gratitude for sharing her editing expertise. Thanks to my Pastors, Morris G. Vaagenes and Robert Burmeister, for their suggestions and comments.

Contents

Preface

This book was written to inform believers what it means to be baptized in the Holy Spirit. My husband, Don, and I have taught classes on this subject since the early 1970s. Throughout the years, we have encountered many comments and questions about the Holy Spirit. This is an attempt to provide some explanations and answers. Because of the many misconceptions about the experience of being baptized in the Holy Spirit, we felt there was a need for material that would be helpful to the body of Christ in understanding this encounter with the Holy Spirit.

This was written also for believers who lack understanding of the passages of Scripture that pertain to the gift of the Holy Spirit. I trust that the explanations of Scripture given will be helpful for private study or group discussion. Selected words in bold in the Scripture passages are for emphasis. Words that are in parentheses in the Scripture passages are mine.

It is my prayer that this book will be of benefit to believers who are seeking this experience or need guidance to pray for others who want the power of the Holy Spirit.

In the title and throughout this book, the preposition *in* is used when referring to the experience of being baptized in the Holy Spirit. In the original Greek text, the word is *en*, and is translated as *in, with*, or *by* in various translations of the Bible. Although many Bible translations use the preposition *with*, the *Pocket Interlinear New Testament* edited by Jay P. Green translates *en* as *in* whenever it refers to the experience of being baptized in the Holy Spirit; I have chosen to do the same.

It is my prayer that the Lord will bless and use this book to edify and empower His body, the church, so that she might attain her high calling in Christ and truly become the witness the Lord has called her to be. To Him be all Glory and Praise!

Elsie Fuhrman

Chapter 1

Born of the Spirit and Baptized in the Holy Spirit

Jesus told His followers that after He had returned to the Father, they would be baptized in the Holy Spirit, which would empower and equip them to be His witnesses throughout the earth (Acts 1:4-8). These words of Jesus came to pass on the day of Pentecost; the disciples were never the same after their encounter with the Holy Spirit. The empowerment of the Holy Spirit is the birthright of every believer. When believers are baptized in the Holy Spirit, they are filled with the Holy Spirit (Acts 2:3-4). The Holy Spirit comes upon them, they are anointed and empowered to serve God, and are given the ability to speak in tongues. The subject of speaking in tongues will be addressed in a later chapter.

Speaking in tongues and being baptized in the Holy Spirit are not essential for salvation. God has one answer for a person's need of salvation—His Son, Jesus Christ. A personal experience of Jesus Christ, the Son of God, acknowledging and confessing Him as the risen Savior and Lord, is salvation. The meaning of the name Jesus in Hebrew is "Jehovah is salvation."

And there is salvation in no one else, for there is no other name under heaven given among men by which we must be saved. Acts 4:12

And this is the testimony, that God gave us eternal life, and this life is in his Son. He who has the Son has life; he who has not the Son of God has not life. 1 John 5:11-12

Our God is a Triune God: God the Father, God the Son, and God the Holy Spirit. The Father and the Son are in heaven. In the Lord's Prayer we say, "Our Father who art in heaven." The Lord Jesus has returned to the Father and is seated at His right hand, a place of ultimate authority and power, making intercession for the saints. The Holy Spirit is the representative of the Godhead *in the earth today;* He has been sent by the Father and the Son to be with, and to indwell believers (John 14:17). Christians should be knowledgeable about the Holy Spirit, because He is the Person of the Godhead at work in their lives. Understanding the fellowship and work of the Holy Spirit enables us to cooperate more fully with Him. The Father and the Son are also with the believer through the Holy Spirit, since our God is one God (Matt. 28:18-20; John 14:10-11, 20, 17:11, 20-23; Mark 12:29).

Being baptized in the Holy Spirit is not a salvation experience, but is a work of God different from, and in addition to, His regenerating work. Neither is being baptized in the Holy Spirit the same as Christian water baptism. A person may be a regenerated baptized believer, but not be baptized in the Holy Spirit.

Baptism in the Holy Spirit is a spiritual experience. To truly understand spiritual life and to grow spiritually, a believer should know that he is a tripartite being. Scripture states there is One Lord, yet our God is Three in One: Father, Son, and Holy Spirit. A person is one entity, yet he is body, soul, and spirit. When God created man, He created him a spirit that possesses a soul and lives in a body. A common misunderstanding is that a person is only soul and body. The unregenerate person, who is not born of the Spirit, does not understand or recognize the spirit side of his nature. In 1 Thessalonians, we find Paul addressing people as spirit, soul, and body.

May the God of peace himself sanctify you wholly; and may your spirit and soul and body be

10

kept sound and blameless at the coming of our Lord Jesus Christ. He who calls you is faithful, and he will do it. 1 Thessalonians 5:23-24

And Mary said, "My **soul** magnifies the Lord, and my **spirit** rejoices in God my Savior." Luke 1:46-47

For the word of God is living and active, sharper than any two-edged sword, piercing to the division of **soul and spirit,** of joints and marrow, and discerning the thoughts and intentions of the heart. Hebrews 4:12

These verses indicate that there is a distinction between the soul and the spirit. If the spirit and soul can be divided, they must be different. In Genesis we find a passage describing God's creation of man as spirit, soul, and body.

And the Lord God formed man of the dust (body) of the ground, and breathed into his nostrils the **breath of life** (spirit); and man became a living **soul.** Genesis 2:7 (KJV)

When God the Creator breathed the "breath of life" into Adam, Adam became alive. In Hebrew the word *life,* as used in "breath of life," is *chay* and is plural. As God breathed the breath of life into Adam, his spirit came into being. As the spirit reacted with Adam's formed body of dust, the soul was created. Adam became a living soul. The breath of life brought forth both spirit and soul. In the books of Job and Ezekiel, we read that the breath of God gives life.

The spirit of God has made me, and the **breath of the Almighty gives me life.** Job 33:4

11

Thus says the Lord God to these bones: Behold, I will cause breath to enter you, and you shall live. Ezekiel 37:5

The word *breath* in the last verse can also be translated as *spirit*. The book of James states that the body without the spirit is dead.

For as the body apart from the spirit is dead, so faith apart from works is dead. James 2:26

An illustration and explanations are given for the differences of the spirit, the soul, and the body in the following paragraphs:

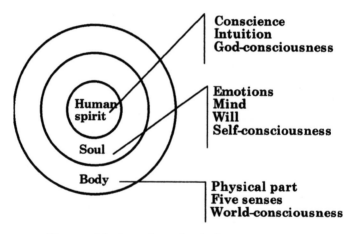

Humankind—tripartite beings

The **spirit** of a person exists independently in the body. When Scripture mentions the inner man (Rom. 7:22; Eph. 3:16; 2 Cor. 4:16), it refers to the spirit and the innermost heart of the person. The human spirit has three functions: conscience, intuition, and communion with God which, though different, are closely entwined. A person's spirit enables him to respond to God because the human spirit has the same nature as God, and therefore can be eternally united with God. This union with God takes place when a person is born of the Spirit; it is only then that a person can have genuine fellowship with God. The spirit, when regenerated, gives the believer a God-consciousness and enables him to commune with God.

Within the human spirit, conscience is the voice of the spirit that distinguishes between right and wrong. When a person is regenerated and born of the Spirit, his conscience is cleansed, and he is able to sense the will of God, and be at peace with God. The believer can then boldly approach the throne of God because he is justified and cleansed from all unrighteousness by the blood of Christ (Heb. 10:19-22; Rom. 3:23-25, 5:9; 1 John 1:7-9). When we sin, the Holy Spirit responds by addressing our conscience, thereby enabling us to repent. When a person repeatedly ignores the voice of his conscience and the Holy Spirit's prompting, the conscience can become seared. A seared conscience is callous, and no longer feels remorse, guilt, or need of repentance.

The intuition of the spirit is independent of outside influence. It provides a sense of "knowing that we know." It is our intuition that receives the revelations and impressions of the Holy Spirit (Rom. 8:16).

Communion with God is possible with our spirit because God is spirit (John 4:24). God's communication with us occurs in the spirit; the spirit is the point of contact between God and believers. Christians are to worship God in spirit and truth. Worshiping God in spirit is honoring Him with heartfelt reverence, devotion, and sincerity with a new spirit and new life. The unregenerate soul is not able to worship God in spirit. A person cannot apprehend God with his thoughts and feelings; neither do rote rituals and rote ceremonies present a spiritual worship of God. When we worship in spirit, we are not relying on the works of the flesh but allowing the Holy Spirit to make our worship sincere and pleasing to God. When our devotion to God is operating in true *scriptural* knowledge of Him, and not as our natural mind or imagination perceives Him, we are worshiping God in truth. The Holy Spirit will cause our love and adoration for God to grow in our hearts, and enable us to magnify and glorify Him in our lives.

For we are the true circumcision, who worship God in spirit, and glory in Christ Jesus, and put no confidence in the flesh. Philippians 3:3

God is spirit, and those who worship him must worship in spirit and truth. John 4:24

The **soul** consists of the mind, emotions, and will. It expresses our individuality, gives us consciousness of our existence and self-awareness, and is the seat of our personality. Our personality is expressed through thoughts, intellect, emotions, feelings, choices, and decisions. The soul of the believer should be governed and ruled by his spirit, which is united with the Holy Spirit. The soul is meant to be the servant of the believer's spirit. The unregenerate person without Christ is governed and ruled primarily by his mind, emotions, and desires of his fleshly appetites (Eph. 2:3).

Within the soul, the mind is the instrument of our thoughts, manifests our intellectual power, and is the reasoning faculty. It is the mind that provides understanding. It needs to be renewed after conversion (Rom. 12:2; 2 Cor. 10:5-6). It is the sanctifying work of the Holy Spirit and obedience to the Word of God that renews the mind by adjusting attitudes and changing values and priorities (Psalms 19:7-11, 119:11, 24, 105). Emotions are the instrument of our likes, dislikes, feelings, and affections. The will, part of the soul, enables us to make choices. God has given humankind free will; He will never take away our right to choose.

The **body** is the physical portion and provides "world-consciousness." The five senses (touch, sight, taste, smell, and hearing) allow us to sense and respond to our environment.

To learn more about the spirit and the soul and how their functions affect our spiritual life, I recommend Watchman Nee's book, *The Spiritual Man*.

Prior to becoming a Christian and being born of the Spirit, the spirit of the unregenerate person is alienated from God (Eph. 4:18). The spirit is defiled, under the power of sin, and in a wretched condition (Rom. 3:9-18). It has lost its spiritual sensibility, is unresponsive to God, and cannot discern spiritual things (1 Cor. 2:14). This person's condition is similar to a dead battery, which needs an outside source to regenerate it.

In their original state, Adam and Eve were able to commune with God because their spirits were undefiled and innocent. Their spirits, through the soul, governed their whole being. When they sinned by disobeying God, their spirits became *dead* to God and their soul became dominant. God had forewarned them that if they disobeyed and ate of the tree of knowledge of good and evil, they would die.

And the Lord God commanded the man, saying, "You may freely eat of every tree of the garden; but of the tree of the knowledge of good and evil you shall not eat, for in the day that you eat of it you shall die." Genesis 2:16-17

Adam and Eve didn't die physically that day, for Adam lived to be 930 years old; but on the day that they ate of the tree of knowledge of good and evil, a death to God entered their spirits, which eventually resulted in physical death. This spiritual death has been passed on to all descendants of Adam and Eve. All are alienated from God until they receive the new life offered to them through the Lord Jesus Christ. This *new life* that is given is God's own life; in Greek the word for this eternal life of God is Zoë. The word *life* appears many times in the New Testament; wherever it is Zoë in Greek, it refers to God's own uncreated life.

Death and spiritual darkness have permeated the spirit, soul, and body of every individual. The spirit of the sinner still exists, but it is dead to God and void of eternal life because of trespasses and sin. There is dire need for the spirit to be cleansed of sin and receive new life (Zoë).

Religious activity and forms of religion cannot take the place of receiving new life. Nicodemus was a religious man, yet to him, Jesus said, "You must be born anew" (John 3:7).

For as in Adam all die, so also in Christ shall all be made alive. 1 Corinthians 15:22

...they are darkened in their understanding, alienated from the life of God because of the ignorance that is in them, due to their hardness of heart. Ephesians 4:18

Without Christ, a person is governed by a mind that is hostile to God (Col. 1:21), and he is unable to understand spiritual things because they are folly and foolishness to him (1 Cor. 1:18, 2:14). We must heed the words of Jesus, "You must be born anew" (John 3:3-7). Unless a person is born anew, he is not able to see (perceive) or enter the kingdom of God.

In the new birth experience, one receives remission of sins, a re-created spirit, and new life (Zoë). How can we receive this new life? How can we be regenerated?

When a person *personally* receives and confesses the Lord Jesus as his Lord and Savior, trusting in His finished work of redemption (1 Cor. 15:1-4) for his salvation, he is saved and regenerated with new life.

Paul explains the New Testament way of salvation in the book of Romans.

...because, if you **confess** with your lips that Jesus is Lord and **believe in your heart** that God raised him from the dead, you will be saved. For man **believes** with his heart and so is justified, and he **confesses** with his lips and so is saved. Romans 10:9-10

...but when the goodness and loving kindness of God our Savior appeared, **he saved us,** not because of deeds done by us in righteousness, but in virtue of his own mercy, by **the washing of regeneration and renewal in the Holy Spirit,** which he poured out upon us richly through Jesus Christ our Savior, so that we might **be justified by his grace** and become heirs in hope of **eternal life.** The saying is sure. Titus 3:4-8

We have this wonderful promise in Romans 10:13: "everyone who *calls* upon the name of the Lord will be saved."

When a person is saved, he is made *alive* with the uncreated eternal life of God (Zoë). God is not a created being; therefore His life is not a created life. He *is* Life (John 14:6); He is the fountain of life. His life is without beginning and without end. There are different kinds of created life, such as plant life, animal life, bird life, and our natural human life (psuche, Gr.), but the life we receive in regeneration is God's own life. This life is in His Son, the Lord Jesus (1 John 5:11-12). Scripture states that in Christ, the believer is a "new creation" (2 Cor. 5:17; Gal. 6:15). The believer becomes a "new species" because he has partaken of the divine nature (2 Peter 1:4), which is Christ indwelling him through the Holy Spirit; Christ in you, the hope of glory (Col. 1:27). Because the Lord Jesus is in heaven with a glorified resurrected body, He comes to us through the Holy Spirit who is called the Spirit of Christ (Rom. 8:9).

And **you he made alive,** when you **were dead** through the trespasses and sins in which you once walked, following the course of this world, following the prince of the power of the air, the spirit that is now at work in the sons of disobedience. Among these we all once lived in the passions of our flesh, following the desires of body and mind, and so we were by nature children of wrath, like the rest of mankind. But God, who is rich in mercy, out of the great love with which he loved us, even when we were dead through our trespasses, **made us alive** together **with Christ** (by grace you have been saved), and raised us up with him, and made us sit with him in the heavenly places in Christ Jesus.
Ephesians 2:1-6

And you, who were dead in trespasses and the uncircumcision of your flesh, **God made alive together with him,** having forgiven us all our trespasses. Colossians 2:13

And this is the testimony, that God gave us eternal life, and **this life is in his Son.** He who **has the Son has life;** he who has not the Son of God has not life. 1 John 5:11-12

Therefore, if any one is in Christ, he is a **new creation;** the old has passed away, behold, the new has come. All this is from God, who through Christ reconciled us to himself...
2 Corinthians 5:17-18

For God so loved the world that he gave his only Son, that **whoever believes in him** should not perish but have **eternal life.** John 3:16

When a person receives Christ, the Holy Spirit takes up residence within him, joining Himself to the believer's spirit (1 Cor. 6:17), becoming one spirit with him. This constitutes being born of the Spirit, regenerated, and having been brought from death to life. He becomes a child of God because he receives the very nature and life of God. The believer is a "wanted child"; he is born of the Spirit because the Father willed it (John 1:12-13).

Everyone who believes that Jesus is the Christ is a child of God. 1 John 5:1

But to all who received him, who believed in his name, he gave power to become children of God; who were born, not of blood nor of the will of the flesh nor of the will of man, but of God. John 1:12-13

...by which he has granted to us his precious and very great promises, that through these you may escape from the corruption that is in the world because of passion, and become partakers of the divine nature. 2 Peter 1:4

The apostle Paul writes in the book of Romans that if we don't have the Spirit of Christ, we don't belong to Christ (Rom. 8:9b). It is the indwelling Spirit of Christ (Holy Spirit) that will give us an assurance and a "knowing" in our spirit that we belong to God.

When we cry, "Abba! Father!" it is the Spirit himself bearing witness with our spirit that we are children of God. Romans 8:16

In 1 Peter 1:23, Peter declares *we have been born anew, not of perishable seed, but of imperishable,* through the living and abiding word of God. Being born of the Holy Spirit is the beginning of the believer's spiritual life—depicted in the following illustration.

Born of the Spirit

But he who is united to the Lord becomes one spirit with him. 1 Corinthians 6:17

Jesus answered him, "Truly, truly, I say to you, unless one is born anew, he cannot see the kingdom of God." Jesus answered, "Truly, truly, I say to you, unless one is born of water and the Spirit, he cannot enter the kingdom of God. That which is born of the flesh is flesh, and that which is born of the Spirit is spirit." John 3:3, 5-6

The book of Proverbs states that our spirit is the lamp of the Lord.

The spirit of man is the lamp of the Lord, searching all his innermost parts. Proverbs 20:27

When we are born of the Spirit, our spirit is quickened as a lamp that has been lit. What oil is to an oil lamp, the Holy Spirit is to the human spirit. Light is now present where there had been spiritual darkness. Jesus said that those who follow Him have the light of life and will not walk in darkness. It is only through the Lord Jesus, the light of the world (John 1:9, 8:12), that people can recognize their lost state and understand the real purpose and meaning of life. Those who respond to Him are rescued from death, spiritual darkness, and Satan's dominion and become children of light (Eph. 5:8; Col. 1:13; Acts 26:18).

Believers have a life relationship with God, for they have the life of God and are sons of God. God is their Father. It was after His resurrection that the Lord Jesus used the phrase "my Father and your Father" (John 20:17). It was His death and resurrection that made it possible for us to become sons of God.

> **For all who are led by the Spirit of God are sons of God.** For you did not receive the spirit of slavery to fall back into fear, but you have received the **spirit of sonship.** When we cry, "Abba! Father!" it is the Spirit himself bearing witness with our spirit that we are **children of God.** Romans 8:14-16

> He destined us in love to be **his sons through Jesus Christ,** according to the purpose of his will, to the praise of his glorious grace which he freely bestowed on us in the Beloved.
> Ephesians 1:5-6

> And because you **are sons,** God has sent the Spirit of his Son into our hearts, crying, "Abba! Father!" So through God you are no longer a slave but a **son,** and if a son then an heir.
> Galatians 4:6-7

What a glorious privilege to have the Creator indwell created man! Many in the church don't fully comprehend this blessed truth! Perhaps greater effort should be made to make new converts more conscious and knowledgeable of the indwelling Holy Spirit; greater effort should also be made to instruct them in the work of the Holy Spirit. Believers should expect the Holy Spirit to guide them in every facet of their spiritual life, mediating to them all the redemptive benefits they have in Christ (John 16:13-15). He will illuminate the Scriptures to them, for He is the Spirit of truth (John 16:13). A revelation to the believer's heart of the indwelling *Holy* Spirit will intensify his distaste for sin and the godless pleasures of the world, and enable him to walk in greater purity and holiness before God.

The apostle Paul longed for the Corinthian believers to grasp the truth that God's Spirit dwelt in them. Because carnal behavior was quite prevalent in the Corinthian church, Paul repeatedly reminded them that they are the temple of God and that the Spirit indwelling them is *Holy*. He knew that a revelation of this truth would cause them to walk in greater purity.

> Do you not **know** that you are **God's temple** and that **God's Spirit dwells in you?** 1 Corinthians 3:16

> Do you not know that **your body is a temple of the Holy Spirit** within you, which you have from God? You are not your own; you were bought with a price. So glorify God in your body.
> 1 Corinthians 6:19

> For we are the **temple of the living God;** as God said, "I will **live in them** and move among them, and I will be their God, and they shall be my people." 2 Corinthians 6:16b

A *heart* revelation of God's holiness mortifies our carnal nature. When Isaiah beheld God's holiness, he cried, "Woe is me! For I am lost; I am a man of unclean lips, and I dwell in the midst of a people of unclean lips; for my eyes have seen the King, the Lord of hosts!" (Isa. 6:1-5). The church today needs a greater revelation of the truth of the indwelling *Holy* Spirit!

When Jesus told His disciples that He was returning to the Father, they were sorrowful. Sensing this, Jesus said He wouldn't leave them without help (John 14:16-18). Some versions of the Bible translate His words as "I will not leave you as orphans." He would return in the coming of the Holy Spirit whom He and the Father would send.

Christ has been clothed with the Holy Spirit since His resurrection and, as a result, is with the believer through the Holy Spirit. The Holy Spirit will be a Counselor, Comforter, and Helper, and as the Spirit of truth, He will make Christ's presence real to the believer.

And I will pray the Father, and he will give you another Counselor, to be with you for ever, even the Spirit of truth, whom the world cannot receive, because it neither sees him nor knows him; you know him, for he dwells with you, and will be in you. John 14:16-17

Jesus said it was to their advantage that He leave (John 16:7), because after His departure, the Holy Spirit would come. Physically, the Lord Jesus could be with them only in one place at one time, but through the Spirit, He would always be with them wherever they were.

After He had risen from the dead, the Lord Jesus appeared to His disciples on the evening of His resurrection and established His identity to them by showing His hands and side. After Jesus said to them that He would send them forth just as the Father had sent Him, He did a most remarkable thing; He breathed on them, telling them to receive the Holy Spirit.

Jesus said to them again, "Peace be with you. As the Father has sent me, even so I send you." And when he had said this, he breathed on them, and said to them, "Receive the Holy Spirit." John 20:21-22

When the Lord Jesus breathed on His disciples, they were born of the Spirit and regenerated with the resurrection life of Christ. As God breathed on Adam to give him life, so the Lord Jesus breathed on the disciples to give them eternal life. At this time, they were born of God and, with this new life came the commission and the legal authority of the Holy Spirit to minister to others. The Holy Spirit is often referred to as the Breath of God; He is the Giver of life. Genesis 2:7 and Job 33:4 state that the breath of the Almighty God gives life. In Greek, the word *pneuma* means both spirit and breath. In 1 Corinthians 15:45, Jesus is spoken of as a life-giving spirit.

The next encounter with the Holy Spirit for the disciples was on the day of Pentecost when they were baptized in the Holy Spirit, receiving power to carry out the authority given to them, and to be witnesses unto the Lord.

Being born of the Spirit and baptized in the Holy Spirit are distinct experiences. Baptism in the Holy Spirit is also distinct from Christian water baptism.

The Greek word for baptize is *baptizo*. It means to immerse, to submerge (as a sunken ship), to cleanse by dipping or submerging, to make clean with water, to overwhelm. God wants us to be immersed, overwhelmed, "waterlogged with the Holy Spirit."

Once a believer is born of the Spirit, he becomes a candidate for baptism in the Holy Spirit, wherein the Holy Spirit comes upon him and empowers him to serve God (Luke 24:49; Acts 1:8).

The following illustration gives a depiction of baptism in the Holy Spirit. The believer is filled and anointed with the Holy Spirit, immersed in the Holy Spirit.

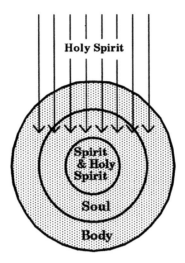

Baptized in the Holy Spirit

When a person is baptized in the Holy Spirit, he receives the same Holy Spirit that came upon the Lord Jesus that empowered and anointed Him for ministry (Mark 1:10; Acts 10:38). The Spirit-filled believer can and should expect the Holy Spirit to work in and through him in a supernatural way. In His timing and at His leading, God will provide opportunities for the Spirit-filled believer to witness and minister.

Jesus said His followers would do the same works that He did and even greater works. Since the Lord Jesus did His work and ministry in the power of the Holy Spirit (Acts 10:38; Luke 4:18), we can presume that the church needs the anointing and power of the Holy Spirit to do the greater works.

"Truly, truly, I say to you, he who believes in me will also do the works that I do; and greater works than these will he do, because I go to the Father. John 14:12

Chapter 2

The Promise of the Father

In the Old Testament, the prophet Joel prophesied that the time would come when God would pour out His Spirit upon His people. The words "pour out" communicate the concept of "the Holy Spirit coming upon."

> **"And it shall come to pass afterward, that I will pour out my spirit on all flesh; your sons and your daughters shall prophesy, your old men shall dream dreams, and your young men shall see visions. Even upon the menservants and maidservants in those days, I will pour out my spirit."** Joel 2:28-29

Joel's prophecy came to pass on the day of Pentecost. This prophetic word has been fulfilled periodically throughout church history and will continue to be fulfilled. God will pour out His Spirit on His people wherever He finds willing and hungry hearts. John the Baptist proclaimed Jesus as the one who baptizes believers in the Holy Spirit. We find this proclamation in all four Gospels.

> **John answered them all, "I baptize you with water; but he who is mightier than I is coming, the thong of whose sandals I am not worthy to untie; he will baptize you with the Holy Spirit and with fire."** Luke 3:16

> **"I baptize you with water for repentance, but he who is coming after me is mightier than I, whose sandals I am not worthy to carry; he will baptize you with the Holy Spirit and with fire."** Matthew 3:11

"I have baptized you with water; but **he will baptize you with the Holy Spirit.**" Mark 1:8

John also proclaimed that Jesus was the Lamb of God who takes away the sin of the world. He is to be received as Savior and as the One who baptizes in the Holy Spirit.

The next day he saw Jesus coming toward him, and said, "Behold, the Lamb of God, who takes away the sin of the world!" John 1:29

I myself did not know him; but he who sent me to baptize with water said to me, "He on whom you see the Spirit descend and remain, this is he who baptizes with the Holy Spirit." John 1:33

In His final words to His disciples before His ascension, Jesus said that they would preach repentance and forgiveness of sins in His name to all nations. He would not require them to do this in their own strength and in their own abilities. He instructed them to remain in Jerusalem, and wait for the promise of the Father that would come upon them and *clothe* them with power!

Then he opened their minds to understand the scriptures, and said to them, "Thus it is written, that the Christ should suffer and on the third day rise from the dead, and that repentance and forgiveness of sins should be preached in his name to all nations, beginning from Jerusalem. You are witnesses of these things. And behold, I send the promise of my Father upon you; but stay in the city, until you are clothed with power from on high." Luke 24:45-49

In the book of Acts, Jesus identifies the promise of the Father as baptism in the Holy Spirit.

And while staying with them he charged them not to depart from Jerusalem, but to wait for the promise of the Father, which, he said, "you heard from me, for John baptized with water, but before many days you shall be baptized with the Holy Spirit." Acts 1:4-5

This encounter with the Holy Spirit would equip and empower them to be His witnesses.

"But you shall receive power when the Holy Spirit has come upon you; and you shall be my witnesses in Jerusalem and in all Judea and Samaria and to the end of the earth." Acts 1:8

The word *power* in this verse can also be translated *ability*. Being baptized in the Holy Spirit gives believers the ability to be witnesses to the risen Christ. This was certainly true for the disciples after they were baptized in the Holy Spirit.

And with great power the apostles gave their testimony to the resurrection of the Lord Jesus, and great grace was upon them all. Acts 4:33

The promise of the Father came at God's appointed time. The disciples and other followers of Jesus were gathered in an upper room in Jerusalem, praying and waiting. The Holy Spirit came upon them powerfully and suddenly in a most unusual way!

When the day of Pentecost had come, they were all together in one place. And suddenly a sound came from heaven like the rush of a mighty

**wind, and it filled all the house where they were
sitting. And there appeared to them tongues as
of fire, distributed and resting on each one of
them. And they were all filled with the Holy Spirit
and began to speak in other tongues, as the
Spirit gave them utterance.** Acts 2:1-4

The Holy Spirit came with the sound of rushing wind,
and visible signs such as tongue-like fires rested upon the
disciples! He came upon the followers of Jesus, filling them
and the room where they were gathered. They began to
speak in tongues and glorify God with utterances given
them by the Spirit! They were baptized in the Holy Spirit
and empowered to serve the Lord!

Upon Jesus, the Holy Spirit came as a gentle dove
(Matt. 3:16), but on these imperfect men, He came as wind
and fire, symbolizing God's power and His purifying work.
The "tongues as of fire" resting on each one indicated that
this was an individual experience from God. The entire
event was a mighty demonstration of God's presence and
power!

Evidently the followers of Jesus, upon whom the Holy
Spirit had come so powerfully, spilled into the public arena
speaking in tongues and declaring the mighty works of God.
Perhaps the tongue-like fires were still upon them, creating
such an unusual sight that it caused a crowd to gather. The
Jews in Jerusalem were astonished and bewildered at this
phenomenon. They were amazed that these unlearned
Galileans were speaking of God and glorifying Him in many
languages. The disciples were so filled with the Holy Spirit
that the crowd accused them of being intoxicated. Peter said
that they were not drunk, but that God had poured out His
Spirit upon them, and filled them with the Holy Spirit!

The tongues spoken by the disciples were a supernatural
sign (Mark 16:17) given by God thereby causing the
multitude to gather; God wanted them to hear Peter speak
about the risen Lord Jesus.

Peter told the crowd in Jerusalem that the prophet Joel had prophesied this outpouring of the Holy Spirit.

And in the last days it shall be, God declares, that I will pour out my Spirit on all flesh, and your sons and your daughters shall prophesy, and your young men shall see visions, and your old men shall dream dreams; yea, and on my menservants and my maidservants in those days I will pour out my Spirit; and they shall prophesy. Acts 2:17-18

Peter then explained to the Jews that they had crucified and killed Jesus of Nazareth who had done mighty works and wonders in their midst. But that God had resurrected Him from the dead and He was alive! It was because of His resurrection and exaltation at the right hand of the Father that the Holy Spirit was poured out upon them. Peter exhorted the crowd to believe in the Lord Jesus who was the Christ, the Anointed One, and their Messiah (Acts 2:22-36).

This Jesus God raised up, and of that we all are witnesses. Being therefore exalted at the right hand of God, and having received from the Father the promise of the Holy Spirit, he has poured out this which you see and hear. Acts 2:32-33

Let all the house of Israel therefore know assuredly that God has made him both Lord and Christ, this Jesus whom you crucified. Acts 2:36

Upon hearing Peter's words, the crowd came under great conviction. The Holy Spirit revealed to their hearts that they had crucified the Messiah, the One who had come to be their King and Redeemer! Their hearts stung with this revelation! They cried out, "What shall we do?" Peter, speaking words of hope, said that if they would repent of their sins and be baptized in the name of Jesus Christ, they would receive the gift of the Holy Spirit. That day, three thousand people were baptized in His name and became followers of Jesus. It was the anointing of the Holy Spirit upon the words of Peter that caused such great conviction to come upon the people.

Now when they heard this they were cut to the heart, and said to Peter and the rest of the apostles, "Brethren, what shall we do?" And Peter said to them, "Repent, and be baptized every one of you in the name of Jesus Christ for the forgiveness of your sins; and you shall receive the gift of the Holy Spirit. For the promise is to you and to your children and to all that are far off, every one whom the Lord our God calls to him." Acts 2:37-39

So those who received his word were baptized, and there were added that day about three thousand souls. And they devoted themselves to the apostles' teaching and fellowship, to the breaking of bread and the prayers. Acts 2:41-42

Before they were baptized in the Holy Spirit, the disciples were weak and frightened men. At the Garden of Gethsemane, Jesus had asked them to watch and pray, but they were unable to stay awake and fell asleep. When the soldiers came, they forsook the Lord and fled. Peter said that he would die for Jesus and never deny Him, but he denied Him three times (Luke 22:57-59). On occasion, the disciples would argue about their personal positions in the kingdom (Luke 22:24). Neither could they always comprehend the words of Jesus (Mark 9:32; John 8:27, 10:6, 12:16).

That the disciples had received power when the Holy Spirit came upon them is evident in Scripture: They were "clothed with power!"

And fear came upon every soul; **and many wonders and signs** were done through the apostles. Acts 2:43

Now many signs and wonders were done among the people by the hands of the apostles. And they were all together in Solomon's Portico. None of the rest dared join them, but the people held them in high honor. **And more than ever believers were added to the Lord, multitudes** both of men and women, so that they even carried out the sick into the streets, and laid them on beds and pallets, that as Peter came by at least his shadow might fall on some of them. The people also gathered from the towns around Jerusalem, bringing the sick and those afflicted with unclean spirits, and **they were all healed.** Acts 5:12-16

Wherever the disciples went, signs and wonders followed. When the lame man, who begged at the gate of the temple, was healed (Acts 3:4-9), the people were amazed! They knew he had been lame since birth and now he was walking, leaping, and praising God. This miracle allowed Peter to witness to the resurrected Lord, explaining that it was by faith in the Lord Jesus that the man was healed. Peter's words and the manifestation of God's healing power allowed many to hear the word of salvation—a multitude of new believers was the result!

But many of those who heard the word believed; and the number of the men came to about five thousand. Acts 4:4

It was the Holy Spirit who gave the disciples such boldness. No longer were they timid and frightened. Even though they were told by the religious leaders not to speak or teach in the name of Jesus, they could not be silenced.

Demonstrations of the power of God continued to follow them.

> **But Peter and John answered them, "Whether it is right in the sight of God to listen to you rather than to God, you must judge; for we cannot but speak of what we have seen and heard."** Acts 4:19

> **"And now, Lord, look upon their threats, and grant to thy servants to speak thy word with all boldness, while thou stretchest out thy hand to heal, and signs and wonders are performed through the name of thy holy servant Jesus." And when they had prayed, the place in which they were gathered together was shaken; and they were all filled with the Holy Spirit and spoke the word of God with boldness.** Acts 4:29-31

Wherever they went, their bold witness upset the status quo. In Acts 16:20 the disciples were accused of disturbing the city! In Acts 17:6 they were labeled as men who turned the world upside down!

All believers can receive this power to witness and serve the Lord, for the gift of the Holy Spirit is promised to everyone God calls to Himself (Acts 2:39). The word "gift" implies something given freely, not earned; but a gift needs to be received. To be a recipient of a gift, we must receive it. Similarly, the Holy Spirit has been sent, but He needs to be received by believers.

It is helpful to understand the gift of the Holy Spirit as twofold. Believers have the indwelling Holy Spirit that they receive upon conversion. It is the indwelling Spirit that imparts new life to them; and the outcome of this Christ-life within is the fruit of the Spirit (Gal. 5:22-23), characteristic of the Lord Jesus. It is the Holy Spirit that conforms believers to the image of the Lord Jesus (Rom. 8:29).

I am the vine, you are the branches. He who abides in me, and I in him, he it is that bears much fruit, for apart from me you can do nothing. John 15:5

But the fruit of the Spirit is love, joy, peace, patience, kindness, goodness, faithfulness, gentleness, self-control; against such there is no law. Galatians 5:22-23

Secondly, believers can also be baptized in the Holy Spirit. In this experience, the Holy Spirit comes upon the believers, imparts the power and anointing of the Holy Spirit, equipping them to witness and minister. This encounter with the Holy Spirit provides the anointing for the supernatural Gifts of the Holy Spirit (1 Cor. 12:7-10) to manifest through believers.

An imperfect analogy of this twofold gift of the Holy Spirit is that when we drink water from a glass, the water is in us. When we walk under a waterfall, the water comes upon us so that we are immersed in water from above. We can have the Holy Spirit indwelling us, and we can be baptized (immersed) in the Holy Spirit.

Just as the indwelling Holy Spirit reproduces the life of Jesus in us, so the Holy Spirit poured out upon us empowers us to minister and witness. The Holy Spirit is God, omnipresent, omniscient, and omnipotent; therefore He can be *in* all believers and also be *upon* them.

Chapter 3

A Promise to All Believers

Approximately 120 followers of Jesus were baptized in the Holy Spirit on the day of Pentecost. According to Scripture, this wasn't the only time the Holy Spirit came upon believers in the New Testament era; others in the early church were also baptized in the Holy Spirit. This promise of the Father was not only for the New Testament church but is for all who follow in the faith.

For the promise is to you and to your children and to all that are far off, every one whom the Lord our God calls to him. Acts 2:39

When the apostles at Jerusalem became aware of the evangelizing work of Philip in Samaria, they were not content to leave these new converts without the power of the Holy Spirit. They sent Peter and John to pray for them to be filled with the Holy Spirit. They had been baptized in the name of the Lord Jesus but had not yet received the power of the Holy Spirit. Peter and John's trip to Samaria allows us to assume that the apostles believed it was important for new believers to receive the power of the Holy Spirit.

Now when the apostles at Jerusalem heard that Samaria had received the word of God, they sent to them Peter and John, who came down and prayed for them that they might receive the Holy Spirit; for it had not yet fallen on any of them, but they had only been baptized in the name of the Lord Jesus. Then they laid their hands on them and they received the Holy Spirit. Acts 8:14-17

It was evident that these new believers received the Holy Spirit. When Simon, a popular magician in Samaria, saw that the Holy Spirit was given with the laying on of hands, he asked to purchase this *power* so that he could lay hands on others to receive the Holy Spirit. Peter, of course, rebuked him, saying that the gift of God could not be bought (Acts 8:18-21). The apostles went to many Samaritan villages preaching the resurrection of the Lord Jesus, and although Scripture does not state it, we can surmise that they also prayed for them to receive the Holy Spirit.

Acts 10:44-48 is an account of the Holy Spirit coming upon the first Gentile converts. The Holy Spirit told Peter, through visions (Acts 10:9-16), that those who were unclean, God had now cleansed. Peter didn't fully understand that the Holy Spirit was speaking about Gentiles. The understanding came later when the Holy Spirit told him to go to the house of Cornelius, a God-fearing Gentile, who had no knowledge of the resurrected Lord Jesus. An angel had previously spoken to Cornelius that he should send for Peter, who would tell him how he and his household might be saved (Acts 11:13-14). Peter, in obedience, went to Cornelius' house, where a large group had gathered. While he was speaking, the Holy Spirit sovereignly came upon all those present.

While Peter was still saying this, the **Holy Spirit fell on all** who heard the word. And the believers from among the circumcised who came with Peter were amazed, because the **gift of the Holy Spirit had been poured out** even on the Gentiles. For they heard them speaking in tongues and extolling God. Then Peter declared, "Can any one forbid water for baptizing these people who have received the Holy Spirit just as we have?" And he commanded them to be baptized in the name of Jesus Christ. Then they asked him to remain for some days. Acts 10:44-48

The Jewish believers who were with Peter were amazed that the Holy Spirit came upon the Gentiles just as He had come upon them at Pentecost! They believed that salvation was for Jews only! As the Gentile converts began to worship God and speak in tongues, Peter realized that since God had indeed brought salvation and the power of the Holy Spirit to them, they also needed to be baptized in the name of the Lord Jesus (water baptism). Scripture states that he remained with them several days, we assume, to instruct and baptize them. When Peter returned to Jerusalem and reported that the Holy Spirit had come upon the Gentiles, some Jews, known as the circumcision party, criticized him for going to the Gentiles (Acts 11:1-18). But others praised God for bringing salvation to the Gentiles.

> **"As I began to speak, the Holy Spirit fell on them just as on us at the beginning. And I remembered the word of the Lord, how he said, 'John baptized with water, but you shall be baptized with the Holy Spirit.' If then God gave the same gift to them as he gave to us when we believed in the Lord Jesus Christ, who was I that I could withstand God?" When they heard this they were silenced. And they glorified God, saying, "Then to the Gentiles also God has granted repentance unto life." Acts 11:15-18**

When the apostle Paul arrived at Ephesus, he met some disciples. He asked them if they had received the Holy Spirit when they believed, which indicates that this was an important aspect of being a disciple. According to Scripture, their knowledge of the Lord Jesus and Pentecost was incomplete. They knew only the message of John the Baptist and his baptism. After Paul instructed them, he baptized them in the name of the Lord Jesus (water baptism). Then laying his hands on them, he prayed for them, and they received the Holy Spirit and began to speak in tongues and prophesy.

> **While Apollos was at Corinth, Paul passed through the upper country and came to Ephesus. There he found some disciples. And he said to them, "Did you receive the Holy Spirit when you believed?" And they said, "No, we have never even heard that there is a Holy Spirit." And he said, "Into what then were you baptized?" They said, "Into John's baptism." And Paul said, "John baptized with the baptism of repentance, telling the people to believe in the one who was to come after him, that is, Jesus." On hearing this, they were baptized in the name of the Lord Jesus. And when Paul had laid his hands upon them, the Holy Spirit came on them; and they spoke with tongues and prophesied.** Acts 19:1-6

These passages of Scripture indicate that in the apostolic age, it was not unusual for believers to be baptized in the Spirit shortly after or at the time of conversion. New converts received not only eternal life but also the power and anointing of the Holy Spirit.

Throughout the New Testament era, the early church moved in the power of the Holy Spirit, which is certainly true of the ministry of the apostle Paul. He was filled with the Holy Spirit through the ministry of Ananias, and received his call and anointing to preach the gospel, which was confirmed with manifestations of the power of the Holy Spirit (Acts 9:11-18).

> **...for our gospel came to you not only in word, but also in power and in the Holy Spirit and with full conviction.** 1 Thessalonians 1:5

Paul did not rely on man's wisdom and abilities to bring people to Christ. He wanted the believers' faith to be anchored in the power of God rather than in the wisdom of man. Paul writes in 1 Corinthians 4:20, "the kingdom of God does not consist in talk but in power."

...and my speech and my message were not in plausible words of wisdom, but in demonstration of the Spirit and of power, that your faith might not rest in the wisdom of men but in the power of God. 1 Corinthians 2:4-5

While on earth, the Lord Jesus was not omnipresent, omnipotent, or omniscient, for He had voluntarily laid aside His power and glory as the Son of God. He came in the likeness of man, as a humble servant. Jesus' entire ministry of miracles, healing, signs, and wonders was done by the power of the Holy Spirit flowing through Him. He was the Divine Son of God, but ministered as a man filled with the Holy Spirit. Jesus relied completely upon the Holy Spirit and the Father (John 5:19).

Have this mind among yourselves, which is yours in Christ Jesus, who, though he was in the form of God, did not count equality with God a thing to be grasped, but emptied himself, taking the form of a servant, being born in the likeness of men. And being found in human form he humbled himself and became obedient unto death, even death on a cross. Therefore God has highly exalted him and bestowed on him the name which is above every name, that at the name of Jesus every knee should bow, in heaven and on earth and under the earth. Philippians 2:5-10

When John the Baptist baptized Jesus in the Jordan River, the Holy Spirit *came upon* Him in the form of a dove.

41

Now when all the people were baptized, and
when Jesus also had been baptized and was
praying, the heaven was opened, and **the Holy
Spirit descended upon him in bodily form,** as a
dove, and a voice came from heaven, "Thou art
my beloved Son; with thee I am well pleased."
Luke 3:21-22

After the Holy Spirit had come upon Him, Jesus returned
from the Jordan, *full of the Holy Spirit* (Luke 4:1). Then He
was led by the Spirit into the wilderness to be tempted by
the devil. Scripture states that after His temptation, Jesus
returned to Galilee in the *power of the Holy Spirit* (Luke
4:14). It was in Galilee that He went to the synagogue and
began to read from Isaiah (Isa. 61:1).

...and there was given to him the book of the
prophet Isaiah. He opened the book and found
the place where it was written, "The **Spirit of the
Lord is upon me, because he has anointed me** to
preach good news to the poor. He has sent me to
proclaim release to the captives and recovering
of sight to the blind, to set at liberty those who
are oppressed, to proclaim the acceptable year
of the Lord." And he closed the book, and gave it
back to the attendant, and sat down; and the
eyes of all in the synagogue were fixed on him.
And he began to say to them, **"Today** this
scripture has been fulfilled in your hearing."
Luke 4:17-21

Jesus declared that the Holy Spirit was upon Him, that
He was anointed to bring good news of salvation to the lost,
the destitute, the poor, and the spiritually blind—essentially
to the entire lost human race. He came to heal the sick, the

afflicted, and the brokenhearted and to free those who are bound and blinded by the devil (1 John 3:8b).

Jesus had come preaching that the kingdom of God (Mark 1:14) was at hand! The Holy Spirit empowered Him to establish the kingdom of God. His works and miracles were evidence that the kingdom of God had come. Wherever Jesus or His disciples taught or preached the gospel of the kingdom, people were healed and miracles took place (Matt. 9:35, 10:7-8; Luke 10:9). Jesus claimed that He, indeed, fulfilled the prophecy spoken by Isaiah many years before (Isa. 61:1).

It was ordained that the Lord Jesus would be the pattern for His church. He would minister under the same conditions as His followers—by the Spirit of God!

...how God anointed Jesus of Nazareth with the Holy Spirit and with power; how he went about doing good and healing all that were oppressed by the devil, for God was with him. Acts 10:38

The Lord Jesus has not changed; He will do the same things today that He did while on earth, but now He chooses to do them through His body, the church. If the church is to do the Lord's work, she too needs to proclaim as Jesus did, "The Spirit of the Lord is upon me!"

The Lord Jesus is now the resurrected and exalted Christ Jesus. The title *Christ* in Greek means *"the Anointed One."* In Paul's epistles, he speaks of Jesus as Christ Jesus, Lord Jesus Christ, or Christ. The Hebrew word *Messiah* also means "the Anointed One." The Lord Jesus is the Anointed One sent from God! Israel today is still looking and waiting for the "Anointed One," and does not recognize that Jesus is the Messiah.

Let all the house of Israel therefore know assuredly that God has made him both Lord and Christ, this Jesus whom you crucified. Acts 2:36

Because the *Head* of the church is Christ the Anointed One, the *body* of Christ (church) is anointed also. The word *Christian* implies "anointed one."

Every member of the body of Christ (church) has a place and a function. In 1 Corinthians 12:12-27, Paul likens the church to a physical body that has many members. Every member of a physical body has a special function, so it is with the body of Christ. One may assume that every member of the body of Christ needs the empowerment of the Holy Spirit to do the work to which he is called. Our physical body needs every member to function properly, as does the body of Christ, the church.

In the Old Testament, the Holy Spirit came upon some of God's people to empower them, but He did not indwell them, because the Lord Jesus had not yet died for the forgiveness of sins. Those whom God chose for specific tasks, such as prophets, kings, judges, and priests, were anointed with holy oil (Exod. 30:25-32). Being anointed with oil signified they were set apart for service to the Lord. The oil was poured on their heads and would run down onto their garments. The word *oil* in Scripture typifies the Holy Spirit. It was the Holy Spirit that enabled these chosen people to perform their duties. For instance, in Exodus 30:25-30, Aaron was anointed with oil to serve as priest. When the oil was poured upon King David, the Spirit of God came upon him. It was the Holy Spirit that empowered Samson and Gideon in their great exploits.

> Then Samuel took the horn of oil, and anointed him in the midst of his brothers; and the **Spirit of the LORD came mightily upon David** from that day forward. 1 Samuel 16:13

> ...the **Spirit of the LORD came mightily upon him (Samson),** and the ropes which were on his arms became as flax that has caught fire, and his

bonds melted off his hands. And he found a fresh jawbone of an ass, and put out his hand and seized it, and with it he slew a thousand men. Judges 15:14-15

And the **Spirit of the LORD** came mightily upon him, and he tore the lion asunder as one tears a kid; and he had nothing in his hand. Judges 14:6

But the **Spirit of the LORD** came upon Gideon, and he blew a trumpet; and Abiezer was gathered after him. Judges 6:34 (KJV)

In this present age of grace, the Holy Spirit indwells all believers and will also come upon them, anointing and empowering them for ministry. This is possible because of the death, resurrection, and exaltation of the Lord Jesus. Scripture states that all believers are considered priests before God.

...and like living stones be yourselves built into a spiritual house, to be a **holy priesthood,** to offer spiritual sacrifices acceptable to God through Jesus Christ. 1 Peter 2:5

But you are a chosen race, a **royal priesthood,** a holy nation, God's own people, that you may declare the wonderful deeds of him who called you out of darkness into his marvelous light. 1 Peter 2:9

...and made **us a kingdom,** priests to his God and Father, to him be glory and dominion for ever and ever. Amen. Revelation 1:6

Believers do not need a human priest to intercede on their behalf. There is one mediator between God and persons and that is Christ Jesus (1 Tim. 2:5; Heb. 4:15).

When the curtain in the temple was torn from top to bottom (Matt. 27:51) at the time of Christ's death, it signified that the way was now open for all to come boldly into the presence of God.

Therefore, brethren, since we have confidence to enter the sanctuary by the blood of Jesus, by the new and living way which he opened for us through the curtain, that is, through his flesh, and since we have a great priest over the house of God, let us draw near with a true heart in full assurance of faith, with our hearts sprinkled clean from an evil conscience and our bodies washed with pure water. Hebrews 10:19-22

The word *sanctuary* indicates the presence of God. We can come boldly and with confidence into the presence of God because we have been justified by the blood of Christ and, through faith, have been made righteous in His sight (Rom. 3:22-25, 5:9; 1 Cor. 1:30). There is no need for a human intermediary, because now we have the priesthood of believers.

As the priests in the Old Testament were anointed with oil to set them apart to do their task, so now all New Testament believers (priests) are to be anointed with the Holy Spirit to do their task.

Chapter 4

Ask and You Will Receive

It is important to know that it is the will of God for His people to be baptized in the Holy Spirit, because faith to receive comes in knowing God's will. In the following verses of Scripture, we find that it is the Father's desire and delight to give the Holy Spirit.

"And I tell you, Ask, and it will be given you; seek, and you will find; knock, and it will be opened to you. For every one who asks receives, and he who seeks finds, and to him who knocks it will be opened. What father among you, if his son asks for a fish, will instead of a fish give him a serpent; or if he asks for an egg, will give him a scorpion? If you then, who are evil, know how to give good gifts to your children, how much more will the heavenly Father give the Holy Spirit to those who ask him!" Luke 11:9-13

Jesus proclaimed that it is the Father's will to give the Holy Spirit and, if we ask, we will receive. God is true to His promises! If we have received the Lord Jesus as our Savior and are walking in the light, we need not fear to ask for the Holy Spirit. We can trust our Heavenly Father to give good things to His children (Matt. 7:11). He will not give us a serpent if we ask for fish! When we ask, we need not plead either, for God will respond to the prayer of faith. Repetitious pleading is unbelief. God's word is the only source of faith (Rom. 10:17 KJV). What has God said in His word? He will give the Holy Spirit to those who ask! Faith believes that if we ask for the Holy Spirit, we will receive Him. Our God is faithful (Gal. 3:2, 5).

Among some believers there is an inordinate fear that if they ask to be baptized in the Holy Spirit, they might be spiritually deceived and receive something demonic. This fear of deception causes some to reject the experience of Holy Spirit baptism. One of Satan's greatest achievements has been to instill a fear of deception into the hearts of God's people, thereby preventing them from seeking the power of the Holy Spirit. We can trust that our Heavenly Father will not abandon us to the whims of the devil. God is our refuge, our fortress, and our Good Shepherd. If we ask for the gift of the Holy Spirit in the name of the Lord Jesus, we should have the courage of faith to believe that we will receive the Holy Spirit and not something from the realm of Satan.

Frequently believers feel unworthy to receive the Holy Spirit. Receiving the gift of the Holy Spirit is not based on human merit, but on the work of the Lord Jesus. Believers can be baptized in the Holy Spirit because of His death, resurrection, and exaltation (John 7:39). They need not attain to a specific level of spirituality before they can receive. It is by His grace that we receive the *gift* of the Holy Spirit.

Occasionally we hear Christians say, "If God wants to baptize me in the Holy Spirit, He knows where I live and He can give it to me." This attitude is not scriptural. The Holy Spirit cannot be received if a negative or passive attitude is present. Jesus said, "If any one thirst, let him come to me and drink"—this He said about the Spirit (John 7:37-39). Scripture explains that all were made to drink of one Spirit (1 Cor. 12:13). To drink implies our participation; we cannot drink unless we choose to do so, nor can we drink with a closed mouth! God cannot fill us with His Spirit if we do not actively receive.

In his letter to the Ephesians, Paul exhorts believers to be filled with the Holy Spirit.

And be not drunk with wine, wherein is excess; but be filled with the Spirit; speaking to yourselves

**in psalms and hymns and spiritual songs,
singing and making melody in your heart to the
Lord; giving thanks always for all things unto
God and the Father in the name of our Lord
Jesus Christ.** Ephesians 5:18-20 (KJV)

Translated from Greek, this passage implies, "be continually filled with the Holy Spirit." It is the will of God for us to be filled with the Holy Spirit at all times. Walking in obedience to the Lord, prayer and meditating on the Word, fellowship with the saints, and praising and worshiping the Lord will keep us filled with the Spirit. Singing praises to God in our spiritual language (tongues) will bring us into the presence of God. James 4:8 declares that if we draw near to Him, He will draw near to us. In His presence there is fullness of joy! (Psalm 16:11).

It is the work of the Holy Spirit to reveal the Lord Jesus to us. When we are baptized in the Holy Spirit, we have a greater awareness of the Lord Jesus. This was certainly true for me when I was baptized in the Spirit; Jesus became "real" to me, it was as if He had stepped out of the Bible! The Holy Spirit always focuses on Jesus and glorifies Him.

**When the Spirit of truth comes, he will guide you
into all the truth; for he will not speak on his
own authority, but whatever he hears he will
speak, and he will declare to you the things that
are to come. He will glorify me, for he will take
what is mine and declare it to you. All that the
Father has is mine; therefore I said that he will
take what is mine and declare it to you.** John 16:13-15

The Holy Spirit is the Spirit of truth (John 16:13). He will declare to us the things of the Lord Jesus, who is truth (John 14:6). Scripture states that the Holy Spirit will lead us into truth and the truth will set us free (John 8:32). Truth is not the opinions of the world or what we perceive it to be, but it is what God says it is (Word of God). Not knowing the truth about God and about ourselves often causes us to be bound and hindered in our lives so that we are not free to be the person that God created us to be. We may have difficulty receiving God's love, loving others, and loving ourselves. We may feel unworthy to receive God's love. As the Holy Spirit reveals God's truth to us, we are set free from our inferiority, our guilt, bondage to sin, fears, addictions, anger, and rejection wounds. Having a *heart* revelation of God's love for us (truth) brings healing and freedom. The Holy Spirit brings us into the abundant life the Lord Jesus came to give us (John 10:10).

Being baptized in the Holy Spirit does not mean that we will be free from trials. But having the power of the Holy Spirit provides a greater awareness and assurance of God's presence, which enables us to endure and be victorious in the trials and difficulties of life. We will have a greater passion for prayer and be able to pray with greater effectiveness, for the Spirit will help us pray (Rom. 8:26-27). The Holy Spirit ministers God's grace, His guidance, and His strength to all facets of our Christian life.

If we live by the Spirit, let us also walk by the Spirit. Galatians 5:25

The power of the Holy Spirit is resurrection power! (Rom. 8:11). His work is to testify that the Lord Jesus has been resurrected. Whenever we encounter a manifestation of the power of the Holy Spirit, we know the Lord Jesus is alive, risen from the dead and exalted at the right hand of the Father.

A believer who has not been baptized in the Holy Spirit isn't second-class in the eyes of the Lord. God loves and accepts us wherever we are in our spiritual journey. Everything we receive from God is by His grace. But it is His will that we become knowledgeable of the abundant blessings that He has for us, so we can appropriate and walk in them.

None of us ever "arrive spiritually." God is not finished with us while we're on this earth. The Holy Spirit will give guidance and revelation to believers if they are open and receptive to the things of God.

The doctrine of baptism in the Holy Spirit is troublesome for some believers because of the passage in Ephesians 4:4 which speaks of *one* baptism.

There is one body and one Spirit, just as you were called to the one hope that belongs to your call, one Lord, one faith, one baptism, one God and Father of us all, who is above all and through all and in all. Ephesians 4:4-6

When presented with the truth that all believers can be baptized in the Holy Spirit, Christians often say, "I've been baptized (meaning they have been baptized in water), why do I need another baptism?" The confusion comes with the word "baptism" because it is used to refer to Christian water baptism and to baptism in the Holy Spirit. To avoid this confusion, perhaps we should replace the phrase "baptism in the Holy Spirit" with "being filled with the Holy Spirit," or "receiving the Holy Spirit." In Scripture, the term "baptism in the Holy Spirit" is not found; the experience is usually spoken of in verb form, such as baptizes, baptized, came upon, fell on, receiving, or filled with the Spirit.

To understand Ephesians 4:4-6 more fully, we need to examine those passages in context with chapters 2 and 3 of Ephesians, which call Jewish and Gentile believers to a strong commitment of unity in the Spirit. Jesus broke down the dividing wall of hostility between the two. When we accept the Lord Jesus Christ, we are no longer Jewish or Gentile in the sight of God, but a member of the body of Christ. God has created in Himself *one new man* (Eph. 2:15) in place of two (Jew and Gentile), reconciling them both to God in *one* body through the redemptive work of Christ. Chapter 4 of Ephesians states there is one body, one Spirit, and one baptism, not one for the Jews and another for the Gentiles. In Christ, there is one baptism, one Spirit, and one body.

The one baptism in Ephesians 4:4 refers to Christian water baptism into Christ (Gal. 3:27; Rom. 6:3-4; Col. 2:12). Because God has put us in Christ (2 Cor. 5:17-18), we are recipients of everything Christ offers. Whatever belongs to Him belongs to us, for we are joint heirs with Him (Rom. 8:17; Gal. 4:7). Scripture states that God has blessed us in Christ with every spiritual blessing in the heavenly places (Eph. 1:3). There is one baptism into Christ, but the life we have in Him will unfold many spiritual blessings as we grow in grace, faith, and knowledge of the Lord Jesus. *Baptism in the Holy Spirit* is the realization of one of the spiritual blessings that we have in Christ. No doubt it will take a lifetime, and perhaps eternity, for the Holy Spirit to bring us into all the blessings that we have in Christ.

When believers are baptized in the Holy Spirit, it lessens the importance of denominational affiliations. In most charismatic groups, believers from many denominational backgrounds worship together. The prayer for the church from the heart of Jesus was "that they may be one even as we are one"(John 17:22-23). When the Holy Spirit is allowed to be sovereign in the life of the church, He will accomplish this "oneness" in the body of Christ.

Segments of the church have a concern about baptism in the Holy Spirit, particularly of speaking in tongues, because they fear it will bring dissension and division. Manifestations of the Spirit may be divisive at times. Jesus' presence and His words often brought division (Luke 12:51-53). He said that He didn't come to bring peace but a sword, and a sword divides. The truth (sword of the Spirit, Eph. 6:17) that Jesus spoke was not received by the "spiritual leaders" of that day and caused great conflict and division. His words were contrary to their theology and to the status quo. They constantly tried to silence Him.

"Do not think that I have come to bring peace on earth; I have not come to bring peace, but a **sword**. For I have come to set a man against his father, and a daughter against her mother, and a daughter-in-law against her mother-in-law; and a man's foes will be those of his own household." Matthew 10:34-36

Do you think that I have come to give peace on earth? No, I tell you, but rather **division**. Luke 12:51

Whenever the Spirit of God restores scriptural truth to the church, it will cause dissension and division, because segments of the church will not receive or accept it. This has always been true, resulting in the formation of many church denominations and divisions. Our prideful carnal nature does not like change and takes offense that we may not have all the truth.

Martin Luther's proclamation of the truth of justification by faith created division and dissension. We can be grateful that Luther did not back away from declaring the truth that had been revealed to him. Neither did he compromise the truth. The reformation of the church has not yet been completed. God is still at work building the church (Matt. 16:18); she is not yet without spot, wrinkle, or blemish (Eph. 5:27). One can assume that there is still a need for further revelation of the Word of God (truth) for the church.

Factions and disagreements will occur as the Lord continues to restore the truth of baptism in the Holy Spirit and the gifts of the Spirit. This would not happen if all of God's people were totally yielded and open to the leading of the Holy Spirit. The church pays too high a price for "no dissension and no division" if she denies the truth of baptism in the Holy Spirit, thus depriving her of the power of the Holy Spirit. Many in Israel did not receive the Lord Jesus during His days on earth (John 1:11), neither will every sector of the church receive what the Holy Spirit is doing today.

The word of God (truth), which is the sword of the Spirit, will always divide that which is of God (spirit) and that which is of man (soulish). When the Lord spoke to Paul on the road to Damascus, truth was revealed to him powerfully, resulting in a changed man. Paul *knew* instantly that what he had been doing was of Paul and not of God! (Acts 9:1:9).

For the word of God is living and active, sharper than any two-edged sword piercing to the division of soul and spirit, of joint and marrow, and discerning the thoughts and intentions of the heart. Hebr.4:12

It is grievous when the church allows ignorance, denominational pride, fear of man, and self-pride to quench the power of the Holy Spirit. Many people are lost spiritually, bound by sin and deception, traumatized mentally and emotionally. Others are in need of deliverance from demonic spirits. Only the church has the Word of Life and the authority to deliver, heal, and minister in the name of Jesus. Without the power of the Holy Spirit, the church is limited in doing the ministry that she alone is authorized to do. A Spirit-filled church has the power of the Holy Spirit and can set people free from deception, the bondage of Satan, and the effects of sin in their souls and bodies. Experiencing and seeing the love of God manifested and demonstrated through an empowered church is what will convince the lost! The church desperately needs the anointing of the Holy Spirit!

In Revelation 1:20, the church is likened to a golden lampstand (golden indicates it is of God). A lampstand requires oil to give light. Oil in Scripture typifies the Holy Spirit. The church as God's lampstand must be filled with the Holy Spirit (oil) to be a light in the midst of a dark world. She is to bear testimony to the resurrected Lord Jesus, proclaim that He is the Savior of the world, and witness to the fact that there is salvation in no other name than Jesus Christ. People can only be saved through His work of redemption (Acts 4:12). Jesus said that His followers are the light of the world (Matt. 5:14). As the golden lampstand, the church must let her light shine (testify and witness) so that all people may see the *good works* and give glory to the Father who is in heaven (Matt. 5:16). The witness of the church is not in words alone but also in *good works*. Power evangelism is what wins people to Christ! It takes the power of the Holy Spirit to convict lost sinners! God's will is that no one should perish; He provided the way of salvation through His Son, Jesus Christ. This good news is to be proclaimed by a Spirit-empowered church with signs and wonders following. It is God's intention that His people minister in the supernatural power of the Holy Spirit. In the early church, the supernatural was commonplace; almost every chapter in the book of Acts mentions the supernatural. In chapter 19, it states that God worked extraordinary miracles by the hands of Paul. "Extraordinary miracles" in Greek means "type of miracles that do not happen every day." The fact that these were recorded as not occurring daily allows us to conclude that perhaps ordinary miracles were very commonplace in the early church.

It has been said that to bring a person to salvation in Christ without guiding him into the power of the Holy Spirit is like recruitment into military service without providing adequate weapons.

Chapter 5

Speaking in Tongues

When we are baptized in the Holy Spirit, we receive the ability to speak in tongues. Scripture states it is a sign that follows those who believe (Mark 16:17).

The word *tongues* refers to languages. Speaking in tongues is an archaic way of saying "speaking in languages." If I speak in a German or a Spanish tongue, it means I am speaking that language. The word *tongues* is a biblical word, therefore it will be used throughout this book.

Speaking in tongues is a spiritual exercise; it is speaking a spiritual language that brings us into the realm of the supernatural. When we pray in tongues, our spirit is speaking to God. It is spirit-to-spirit communication. Scripture states that God is spirit (John 4:24).

For if I pray in a tongue, my spirit prays but my mind is unfruitful. What am I to do? I will pray with the spirit and I will pray with the mind also; I will sing with the spirit and I will sing with the mind also. 1 Corinthians 14:14-15

For one who speaks in a tongue speaks not to men but to God; for no one understands him, but he utters mysteries in the Spirit. 1 Corinthians 14:2

God gives us the ability to speak to Him in a spiritual language. Our spirit was created to communicate with God. When we are baptized in the Holy Spirit, our spirit is liberated and speaking in tongues expresses that liberation. Birds fly in the air and fish swim in water, their normal environment; when the believer speaks in tongues, his spirit is in its normal environment. Speaking in tongues is both human and divine and is a cooperation between the believer and the Holy Spirit. When we speak in "everyday" language, the mind controls what is said. When we speak in tongues, our spirit is praying and our mind is not actively involved (1 Cor. 14:14). We are also yielding to God the "unruly, unrighteous member" of our body—the tongue. Our tongue, when speaking out of our old nature, can cause much pain with its verbal abuse, cursing, and speaking of evil and vile things (Rom. 3:13-14). In the book of James it is stated that no man can tame the tongue (James 3:6-10). But in the exercise of speaking in tongues, God brings the tongue into submission and uses it for His purposes and His glory.

On occasion, when a baptized-in-the-Spirit believer speaks in tongues for the first time, one is able to hear and sense the yearning that their human spirit had for expression just by the flow and sound of the spiritual language. As the tongues are uttered, one can perceive the liberation their spirit is experiencing. Speaking in tongues enables the believer to express the inexpressible!

Because there is lack of knowledge and much misinformation in the Christian church about speaking in tongues, many have distorted ideas and misconceptions about this subject. Even the word *tongues* may cause some Christians to become fearful because it provides mental images of fanaticism, frenzied speaking, excess emotionalism, hypnotic trances, or seizures. Speaking in tongues is none of these. It is often labeled as ecstatic utterances. The word *ecstasy* is never associated with tongues in the Bible. Ecstatic speech is not a biblical term, yet it is frequently used in conjunction with speaking in tongues. Some also believe that tongues are just mere babble, anti-intellectual and inappropriate for the church today.

Throughout the history of the church there has been abuse and misuse of the Spiritual Gifts, including speaking in tongues. The carnal actions, foolishness, and ignorance of some have caused others to distance themselves from any manifestations of the Holy Spirit. But rejecting the gifts of the Holy Spirit is not the right response—the right response is to obtain a scriptural understanding of the Gifts and to learn to exercise them properly. If we ask, the Holy Spirit, as the Spirit of truth, will provide insight and revelation regarding speaking in tongues.

In 1 Corinthians 14, the apostle Paul instructs the church at Corinth in the exercise of speaking in tongues. The Corinthian church was a young, immature church, not far removed from paganism and still carnal in worship and lifestyle (1 Cor. 3:1-4, 5:1-2, 11:17-22). They were eager for manifestations of the Spirit (1 Cor. 14:12), but were disorderly in their worship and in the exercise of the Gifts, which caused confusion and division (1 Cor. 11:18, 14:26-33). Apparently many were prophesying and speaking in tongues simultaneously, without waiting for each other. It is probable that tongues uttered in their assemblies were not interpreted (1 Cor. 14:9, 13, 27). The Corinthians did not appear to understand the difference between devotional speaking in tongues and the exercise of the Gift of Various Tongues.

The devotional use of tongues is for the believer's edification (1 Cor. 14:4); the Gift of Various Tongues (1 Cor. 12:10), exercised in an assembly, is for the edification of the corporate body of believers and requires interpretation (1 Cor. 14:9, 27).

In his letter, Paul endeavors to instruct the church in the proper exercise of the gifts. His shepherd heart always longed for the church to be edified and built up. He admonishes them to strive to excel in building up the church (1 Cor. 14:12). He encourages prophecy and tongues with interpretation in the assembly because this will edify the church. Paul is not belittling tongues when he writes that he would rather speak five words with his mind in order to instruct others, than ten thousand words in a tongue (1 Cor. 14:19). He is indicating that the church will only benefit if they understand the messages uttered in tongues. If believers do not receive the interpretation of the tongues uttered in the assembly, then it is better to speak in the vernacular.

Paul also admonishes them to exercise the Gifts of the Spirit in a decent, orderly, and proper manner. God is not a God of confusion, but a God of order and peace. Neither did he intend for them to quench the manifestations of the Spirit, for he tells them not to forbid speaking in tongues. Perhaps Paul knew that churches frequently go "overboard" and quench the manifestations of the Holy Spirit in order to avoid controversy. As for himself, he thanked God that he spoke in tongues more than they did (1 Cor. 14:18). In his letter to the Corinthians, he writes that his instructions to them were a command of the Lord.

When believers are assembled in worship, the tongues spoken in praise and worship to God do not need to be interpreted. During intercessory prayer ministry to the saints, interpretation is not necessary either. Neither does the devotional use of tongues require interpretation.

Some believe that speaking in tongues will cause an uncontrollable emotional outburst that would be embarrassing and appear undignified. God is gentle; He works with us and does not compel us to do anything—whatever is compulsive is not of the Holy Spirit. He always desires our cooperation. He may prompt us, but we must exercise our free will; the decision to speak in tongues is always the prerogative of the believer. We can stop and start at will; it is not an involuntary action. We choose to speak in tongues; God does not compel us to speak! (1 Cor. 14:32). The Holy Spirit has been given to help us, not to make us do something! He will not be unkind to us although on occasion, He may deal with our intellectual pride. There is a humbling aspect to the act of speaking in tongues, for it is necessary to yield and submit to the Holy Spirit. It is always beneficial for us to humble ourselves before the Lord. God exalts and gives grace to the humble, and opposes the proud (1 Peter 5:5-6; James 4:6,10; Matt. 23:11). God dwells with those who have a contrite and humble spirit (Isa. 57:15). Proverbs 15:33 also states that humility goes before honor.

At Pentecost (Acts 2) when the disciples were filled with the Holy Spirit *they began to speak* in tongues as the Holy Spirit gave them utterance. They exercised their will and began to speak as the Holy Spirit gave them words.

And they were all filled with the Holy Spirit and began to speak in other tongues, as the Spirit gave them utterance. Acts 2:4

Speaking in tongues will seem foolish to an unrenewed mind. Speaking a language that we do not understand does not seem beneficial to the reasoning mind. Humankind is mind oriented. When Adam and Eve sinned, their soul, which includes the mind, became dominant and their spirit came under the rule of the soul. This dominance of the soul has been passed on to all their descendants. Western civilization, in particular, tends to deify the intellect. Our natural mind is not inclined to "take the back seat" and allow the spirit to have expression. The carnal natural person who is governed by the mind finds speaking in tongues offensive and foolish (1 Cor. 2:14). But what appears foolish to him is the wisdom of God. Scripture states that the "foolishness of God is wiser than men" (1 Cor.1:25). God, in His great wisdom, gives His people the ability to speak to Him in a spiritual language, beyond the believer's natural understanding. He who speaks in tongues speaks to God (1 Cor. 14:2). God's ways are definitely not our ways; His ways are much higher (Isa. 55:8-9).

Praying in the Spirit can build up our faith. When we find our faith weak and faltering, with doubt and fear tormenting us, that is the time to pray in the Spirit. According to the words of Jude, we can presume it also keeps us aware of the love of God.

But you, beloved, build yourselves up on your most holy faith; pray in the Holy Spirit; keep yourselves in the love of God. Jude 1:20-21

When a believer prays in tongues, he is praying in the Holy Spirit. When the phrase "in the Spirit" is used, it indicates that the Holy Spirit is inspiring, enabling, and administrating the activity. We may also pray in the Spirit in "everyday language" when led by the Holy Spirit.

Speaking in tongues will build up the believer's spirit, thereby aiding him to be governed by his spirit, rather than be ruled by the mind and emotions (soul).

We are edified when we pray in tongues. To edify means to build up and improve. Praying in tongues "charges our spiritual battery." This spiritual exercise allows us to become strong in spirit and sensitive to the things of God. When believers experience spiritually dry times, it is beneficial to pray in their spiritual language.

He who speaks in a tongue edifies himself, but he who prophesies edifies the church.
1 Corinthians 14:4

We can also sing in our spiritual language (1 Cor. 14:15). When we sing in tongues in worship to God, it allows us to praise God beyond our natural abilities. This is a beautiful aspect of our spiritual language. To worship and praise God with other believers in this way is an uplifting, edifying experience. Scripture indicates that God inhabits the praise of His people (Psalm 22:3 KJV); thus, when we praise God with our spiritual language, we are ushered into His presence. It raises us to new heights in praising God! Praise is said to be the "spark plug of faith." If we have difficulty with doubt and unbelief, praising God can be the answer, for it takes our mind off the problem and causes us to focus on God, thus igniting our faith. Praising God can also be a spiritual weapon; the devil flees when God's people praise the Lord (2 Chron. 20:21-23). There is more emphasis on praise than prayer in the Scriptures. In Psalms 148 through 150, David proclaims the entire universe as praising the Creator. "Let everything that breathes praise the Lord!" (Psalm 150:6).

Let the high praises of God be in their throats and two-edged swords in their hands. Psalm 149:6

After experiencing baptism in the Holy Spirit, a friend indicated that she repeatedly found the word "gottleib" in her spiritual language. She was perplexed because "gottleib" was the name of a local business establishment. When she became aware that the word means "God beloved" in German, she was relieved to learn that she was speaking her adoration to God. We do not know whether the tongues that we receive are a language presently known, past, or ancient, but we know it is a language. This was true at Pentecost (Acts 2:8-11). In 1 Corinthians 13, apostle Paul writes about tongues of *men and angels*, so it is possible that at times tongues may be a heavenly language, but we can't be dogmatic about it.

Praying in tongues can benefit those who need healing of emotional or rejection wounds. The painful memories of life's traumas are often suppressed in the deep recesses of the mind and heart. This can have a devastating effect on a person's life, causing great mental anguish, depression, lack of self-esteem, and other difficulties. Consciously they may not always know exactly what the problem or need is, but the Holy Spirit has all knowledge and can enable them to pray for these inner needs. Praying in tongues allows the Holy Spirit to deal with the innermost needs of the heart, thus bringing wholeness, healing, and freedom. Jesus came to heal and bind up those who are brokenhearted and crushed in spirit (Psalms 34:18, 147:3; Isa. 61:1). God desires wholeness for His people.

Praying in tongues gives us greater power and dimension in prayer. Because we have limited knowledge, we do not always know how to pray for others or for a particular situation. It is comforting to know that we can trust the Holy Spirit to direct our spiritual prayer language so that we are praying according to the will of God. We can come into line with God's purposes when we pray in tongues.

Likewise the Spirit helps us in our weakness; for we do not know how to pray as we ought, but the Spirit himself intercedes for us with sighs too deep for words. And he who searches the hearts of men knows what is the mind of the Spirit, because the Spirit intercedes for the saints according to the will of God. Romans 8:26-27

Because believers are involved in spiritual warfare, Paul advocates putting on the whole armor of God and praying at all times in the Spirit.

Finally, be strong in the Lord and in the strength of his might. Put on the whole armor of God, that you may be able to stand against the wiles of the devil. For we are not contending against flesh and blood, but against the principalities, against the powers, against the world rulers of this present darkness, against the spiritual hosts of wickedness in the heavenly places. Therefore take the whole armor of God, that you may be able to withstand in the evil day, and having done all, to stand. Stand therefore, having girded your loins with truth, and having put on the breastplate of righteousness, and having shod your feet with the equipment of the gospel of peace; besides all these, taking the shield of faith, with which you can quench all the flaming darts of the evil one. And take the helmet of salvation,

and the **sword of the Spirit,** which is the **word of God. Pray at all times in the Spirit,** with all prayer and supplication. To that end keep alert with all perseverance, making supplication for all the saints. Ephesians 6:10-18

Spiritual warfare must be waged in the power of the Holy Spirit. Our enemy, the devil, is a spiritual being; Scripture states that we wrestle not against flesh and blood, but against spiritual powers. Praying in tongues is crucial in spiritual warfare because we are limited in comprehending the realm of the enemy. The Holy Spirit is not limited in knowledge and can direct us to pray effectively against our spiritual enemy. Warfare against Satan's spiritual forces may require intensity in prayer that cannot be expressed with our limited natural vocabulary.

The church needs *spiritual* armor and *spiritual* weaponry (Eph. 6:11). The weapons of her warfare are not carnal, but have *divine* power to destroy strongholds (2 Cor. 10:4). Carnal weapons are ineffective against evil spiritual forces.

Throughout church history, the devil has worked diligently and successfully to rob large sectors of the church of the gift of speaking in tongues, because he knows that believers praying in the Spirit are powerful in prayer and effective in destroying his activities.

Speaking in tongues should manifest when a person is baptized in the Holy Spirit. Tongues are the overflow of being filled. Occasionally, the manifestation of tongues comes later. However, if one has been baptized in the Spirit, there will be a desire to speak in tongues and eventually the person will, if instructed properly. There is often a lack of the Holy Spirit's power until one does speak in tongues. Scripture states that when one is baptized in the Holy Spirit, one receives power and speaking in tongues is a way to release that power. When God spoke, His creative power was released! God formed the earth by His spoken word (Genesis 1; Psalm 33:6-9). His Word is the sword of the

Spirit (Eph. 6:17). When we pray in tongues, God's might and power can be brought into the situation.

Believers who have difficulty speaking in tongues may not understand that they have an active part in speaking in tongues. They wait for God to do it all. They've never participated actively and therefore have not spoken in tongues. Upon being filled with the Holy Spirit, the believer should initiate speaking syllable sounds, which the Holy Spirit will perfect into a language. As he initiates sounds, the Holy Spirit will shape the sounds into words. Speaking in tongues is accomplished by faith; we *believe* God will give us this ability and then give *corresponding action* to our faith by speaking. Two events from Matthew are examples of faith with corresponding action (faith with works):

In Matthew 14, we find Peter in a boat and Jesus walking on the water. Peter asks Jesus to bid him to come. Jesus said, "Come!" The only way Peter could come to the Lord was to walk on the water. He had to *believe* that at the word of Jesus, he could do so. He also had to *act* his belief (faith), by stepping out of the boat, and begin to walk. He would not have been able to walk on the water if he hadn't gotten out of the boat and began to take steps. Peter had to do the natural act of walking; God did the supernatural act of keeping him from sinking. Likewise the only way we will ever speak in tongues is to open our mouth and speak (doing the natural), having faith that the Holy Spirit will provide the spiritual language (supernatural).

In Matthew 12:13, Jesus met a man with a withered hand and said to him, "Stretch out your hand!" The man could have said, "I can't, it is withered, heal my hand, then I will stretch it out!" But in obedience he put action to faith by attempting to stretch out his hand and as he did so, he was healed. His faith was completed by his action (James 2:22). His part in the restoration of his hand was providing corresponding action to his faith. The same applies in the exercise of speaking in tongues. As we respond in faith with corresponding action by speaking, the Holy Spirit will do His part and the language will come. Faith is not just passive mental assent, but requires action. When we act upon God's Word, it brings results. Faith without corresponding action (works) is dead as the body is dead without the spirit.

So faith by itself, if it has no works, is dead.
James 2:17

You see that faith was active along with his works, and faith was completed by works.
James 2:22

For as the body apart from the spirit is dead, so faith apart from works is dead. James 2:26

Some believers are so filled when baptized in the Holy Spirit that it appears little faith or action on their part is required; their spiritual language comes bubbling out freely and forcefully. It's as if "rivers of living water" are flowing from their spirit. It would be wonderful if that always occurred, but usually believers need to begin speaking syllable sounds in faith and, as they do, the spiritual language comes forth.

In the initial attempt to speak in tongues, there is a tendency to speak in "everyday" language. People need to be gently reminded that they cannot speak two languages at once. If they speak words that their mind understands, their mind will remain in control and they will be unable to pray with the spirit (1 Cor. 14:14). Speaking in tongues is praying with the spirit, not the mind.

Occasionally believers find their spiritual language lacks fluency, they frequently have a phrase or two that is seemingly repeated over and over. The tendency is to become discouraged and give up speaking in tongues. Repetition of one or two phrases and lack of fluency may occur because they are *thinking* of the words that they are speaking, having more or less memorized them. This makes it a mental exercise instead of a spiritual exercise. Their mind is in control, thus hindering their spirit from speaking fluently. What may be helpful in this situation is to speak rapidly and loudly in the tongues they do have, not giving the mind an opportunity to think of the words. Also, *doubting* that one's tongues are "real" can hinder the fluency of tongues. It is by *faith* we speak. The believer must trust and believe (faith) that what he is speaking in tongues is valid and good! A precious gift from God! Believe! Believe! Believe!

When believers speak in tongues, they are allowing their spirits to have expression. This strengthens and builds up their spirits to become the governing and ruling part of their being, rather than be ruled by their minds, emotions, and fleshly appetites. The spirit of a person can be developed just as the physical body and the intellect (soul) can be. People often spend great sums of money to develop their physical bodies and minds, yet neglect the most important part of their being, the spirit. The natural carnal person, who is not born of the Spirit, and Christians whose actions are still carnal are ruled by their soul (intellect, emotions, self-will) and the desires of their bodies. During the immature stages of a Christian's life after conversion, there is still a tendency for the carnal nature to rule; although Christian, he may still act in a carnal manner. Spiritual persons are those who are governed by their spirits that are united with, and influenced by, the Holy Spirit. Spiritual maturity comes through the sanctifying work of the Holy Spirit and our obedience to Him (Gal. 5:5, 16-22, 25; Rom. 8:13-14). God desires that we become "spiritual men and women" (1 Cor. 2:15, 3:1-3), who live by the Spirit, walk by the Spirit, and are led by the Spirit (Rom. 8:5,14; Gal. 5:16, 25).

Some Christians who do not believe that all believers can have the ability to speak in tongues cite the following Scriptures:

...to another the working of miracles, to another prophecy, to another the ability to distinguish between spirits, to another various kinds of tongues, to another the interpretation of tongues. All these are inspired by one and the same Spirit, **who apportions to each one individually as he wills.** 1 Corinthians 12:10-11

Do all possess gifts of healing? **Do all speak with tongues?** Do all interpret? 1 Corinthians 12:30

When read in context, these passages refer to the Gift of Various Kinds of Tongues (1 Cor. 12:10, 30) that is exercised in an assembly of believers. It does not refer to the personal devotional exercise of tongues. The Gift of Various Kinds of Tongues is a manifestation of the Holy Spirit that prompts a believer to speak a message in tongues in a congregational setting. This is for edification of the corporate body of believers, and requires interpretation. Tongues uttered in this manner are similar to prophecy, a word from God to His people (1 Cor. 14:5). The context of the phrase "Do all speak in tongues?" indicates that not all believers will exercise the Gift of Various Kinds of Tongues in an assembly, only those who are prompted by the Holy Spirit to do so. To help our understanding, we note that all believers can pray for healing for one another, but not all have a healing ministry, manifesting Gifts of Healing (1 Cor. 12:9). All Spirit-filled believers can speak in tongues for their own edification and intercession for others but not all will exercise the Gift of Various Kinds of Tongues in an assembly where interpretation is required.

Many in the church quote 1 Corinthians 13 as implying that tongues have now ceased; that they were only for the apostolic age.

Love never ends; as for prophecies, they will pass away; as for tongues, they will cease; as for

knowledge, it will pass away. For our knowledge is imperfect and our prophecy is imperfect; but when the perfect comes, the imperfect will pass away. 1 Corinthians 13:8-9

For now we see in a mirror dimly, but then face to face. Now I know in part, then I shall understand fully, even as I have been fully understood. 1 Corinthians 13:12

A time will come when prophecy and knowledge will pass away and tongues will cease; that time will be "when the perfect comes." This indicates the end of this age, when Christ, the Perfect One, will come and His church (the body of Christ) will be perfect in knowledge and character (Rom. 8:29-30; Eph. 4:13) for we shall be like Him when we see Him (Phil. 3:20-21; 1 Cor. 15:51-52).

Beloved, we are God's children now; it does not yet appear what we shall be, but we know that when he appears we shall be like him, for we shall see him as he is. 1 John 3:2

Scripture indicates that when we see face to face, we will fully understand, even as we have been understood. The church still sees through a mirror dimly and not face to face (1 Cor. 13:12). The church has not yet come to the place of full understanding; and until that time comes, there is a need for prophecy, knowledge, and tongues.

Some believe that the phrase "when the perfect comes" (1 Cor. 13:10) refers to the completed canon of Scripture, implying that tongues and prophecies have ceased since we have the Scriptures. If this speaks of the completed canon of Scripture, then knowledge would also have passed away and the church would no longer need prophets, teachers, or pastors (1 Cor. 12:28; Eph. 4:11-13). Also, if it refers to the completed canon, we "would understand more clearly" than the apostle Paul. It was to Paul that God revealed the Gospel itself—salvation through the death and resurrection of the Lord Jesus Christ, salvation of the Gentiles and the church as the body of Christ (Gal. 1:11-12; Eph. 3:3-6; 1 Cor. 11:23, 15:1-3; Rom. 16:25; Col. 1:27). The context of 1 Corinthians 13 is love and the Gifts of the Holy Spirit and not the Scriptures; therefore we may assume that this passage does not refer to the completed canon of Scripture.

Some believe that the Bible implies that tongues are the least of the gifts, therefore they are an inferior gift and not worthwhile to consider. They come to this conclusion because "speakers in various kinds of tongues" are listed last in the following Scripture.

Now you are the body of Christ and individually members of it. And God has appointed in the church first apostles, second prophets, third teachers, then workers of miracles, then healers, helpers, administrators, speakers in various kinds of tongues. 1 Corinthians 12:27-28

Because tongues are listed last does not necessarily imply that it is a least gift. When Paul speaks of faith, hope, and love (1 Cor. 13:13), he mentions love last and yet refers to it as the greatest. The fact that speaking in tongues was the first spiritual gift manifested on the day of Pentecost should be evidence that tongues are not inferior or least. Some indicate that speaking in tongues is a lesser gift, citing the following Scripture.

He who prophesies is greater than he who speaks in tongues, unless some one interprets, so that the church may be edified. 1 Corinthians 14:5b

What Paul is implying in this passage is that if messages given in tongues are not interpreted, then prophecy is of more benefit to the church. If there is interpretation, tongues are of equal benefit.

Even if the gift of speaking in tongues is of less significance than other gifts, the church needs everything that God desires to give for her benefit. We should esteem all the gifts of God. Our Heavenly Father gives good things to his children (Matt. 7:11; James 1:17).

Scripture states that tongues can be a sign to the unbeliever:

Thus, tongues are a sign not for believers but for unbelievers, while prophecy is not for unbelievers but for believers. 1 Corinthians 14:22

Speaking in tongues is not a *sign* to the Spirit-filled believer, who knows that it is a valid spiritual exercise; but, to the unbeliever, tongues can be a sign from God. The tongues spoken by the disciples at Pentecost were a sign to the unbelieving multitude (Acts 2:6-12). An utterance in tongues can be a sign of the presence of God for unbelievers when the language is understood and identified by them, thus confronting them with the factuality of God. There have been occasions when unbelievers understood the tongues that were spoken in an assembly; the message given spoke to them of personal matters that were not known by the person who gave the utterance. As a result they were awakened to the reality of God, came under conviction, and received Christ as Savior. When unbelievers mock tongues as mere gibberish and not of God, this very mockery becomes a *sign* of their unbelief.

The ability to pray in tongues is especially beneficial when the Holy Spirit calls believers to intercessory prayer. We may not always understand or comprehend the concern of God's heart, but as we yield to the Holy Spirit and let Him direct our spiritual language, we can be confident that we are interceding according to the will of God (Rom. 8:26-27).

Jesus said that rivers of living water would flow out of the innermost being (spirit) of those who believe in Him.

> **On the last day of the feast, the great day, Jesus stood up and proclaimed, "If any one thirst, let him come to me and drink. He who believes in me, as the scripture has said, 'Out of his heart (spirit) shall flow rivers of living water.'" Now this he said about the Spirit, which those who believed in him were to receive; for as yet the Spirit had not been given, because Jesus was not yet glorified.** John 7:37-39

The phrase, "rivers of living water," represents life that flows from God. The Holy Spirit is the giver of this life (2 Cor. 3:6). Speaking in one's spiritual language allows *living water* to flow from our spirit, renewing and edifying us. In prayer ministry to the saints, it ministers life and blessing. "There is a *river* whose streams make glad the city of God, the holy habitation of the Most High" (Psalm 46:4).

Speaking in tongues edifies believers and promotes their spiritual growth. It enables them to truly praise and worship God in spirit and truth. The natural vocabulary is limited in expressing love and adoration for God. Having the ability to speak in tongues is evidence and assurance to them that they have been baptized in the Holy Spirit and that the Holy Spirit is ever present in their life.

Chapter 6

Prayer to Receive the Holy Spirit

When praying for a person who desires to be baptized in the Spirit, it is essential to know that the person is a Christian and has received the Lord Jesus as Savior. Some may not realize that church membership, living a moral life, and/or having Christian parents does not make one a Christian. If there is a question whether the person has been born of the Spirit, you can lead them in a prayer for salvation. A prayer similar to this one may be used:

Lord Jesus, I confess with my mouth that You are Lord. I declare there is no other name by which I can be saved. I believe You died for the forgiveness of my sins and that You have redeemed me with Your precious Blood. I receive You as my Savior and surrender my life to You. I receive the gift of eternal life offered to me. Thank You for saving me. Come into my life, take my life, and use it for Your glory. Amen.

In our classes, we provide scriptural teaching on baptism in the Holy Spirit and share personal testimony. If any desire to be baptized in the Holy Spirit, we lay hands on them and pray for them to receive the Holy Spirit.

In Scripture, the new birth experience and being baptized in the Holy Spirit are both described as *receiving the Holy Spirit*. The disciples' new birth experience, which occurred on the day of Christ's resurrection, is described as receiving the Holy Spirit (John 20:22). The next two passages of Scripture interpret receiving the Holy Spirit as baptized in the Holy Spirit. In Acts 8: 15-17, Peter and John prayed for the new converts in Samaria to receive the Holy Spirit. In Acts 19:1-7, Paul asks the disciples at Ephesus if they received the Holy Spirit when they believed—whether they had been baptized in the Holy Spirit. In both the new birth experience and baptism in the Holy Spirit, it is the Holy Spirit that is received. The *primary* goal when one is baptized in the Holy Spirit is not to "speak in tongues" or to receive a "baptism" but to receive the Holy Spirit—to be filled with the Holy Spirit. The exercise of speaking in tongues is the overflow of being filled with the Spirit.

After we have prayed for those who desire to be baptized in the Holy Spirit, we lead them to pray a prayer of asking similar to the following:

> Gracious Heavenly Father, I thank You for the promise of the Holy Spirit. Lord Jesus, I declare You are my Savior and Lord. I want to be baptized in the Holy Spirit; I want to be filled with the Holy Spirit. I believe that as I ask, I will receive, because You are faithful to Your Word. I receive (attitude of receiving) the Holy Spirit. I thank You for the gift of the Holy Spirit and I will speak forth in a new tongue to the glory of God. Amen.

After the prayer, we quietly provide opportunity for them to receive the filling of the Holy Spirit. We suggest that they begin to speak in tongues at their discretion, having already instructed them that in order to speak in tongues, it is necessary to begin speaking. They need not think of words, for their mind is to be "unfruitful" at this time. Frequently people just say, "ah, ah, ah, ah, ah," but that is not speaking. It needs to be verbal syllable sounds, moving their lips and tongue. As they do so, the Holy Spirit will give the language. They need not be concerned what it sounds like nor should they speak in everyday language. What it sounds like is the Holy Spirit's prerogative. We usually pray quite audibly in tongues at this time, so that they will not be so inclined to "hear and think" of what they are speaking. They should not imitate another's tongues because the language would not be from their spirit

It is best when believers speak in tongues the first time that they have prayer for baptism in the Holy Spirit, because it is evidence to them that they received the filling of the Spirit and also eliminates any doubts that may come later. If they fail to have the evidence of speaking in tongues, it may be a struggle for them to believe that they really did receive. This lack of assurance can cause them to have fear and doubt that nothing will happen if they should ask again. Frequently the thought of "trying again" brings misgivings and apprehension. When there is failure to speak in tongues, disappointment and discouragement may set in. Hearts may even become hardened after repeated failures. Some conclude that the filling of the Holy Spirit with the ability to speak in tongues was not meant for them and they give up asking and seeking.

We've had some in our classes that had wanted to speak in tongues for many years. Their faith to receive was weak and wavering, because nothing ever seemed to happen when they prayed. Our experience reveals that often persons do not receive instruction to put action to their faith. They weren't aware that if they begin to speak in a childlike act of faith, the Holy Spirit will do His part and tongues will flow! They were waiting for God to do it all.

When a person initially speaks in tongues, it is good to encourage them to believe that the words are genuine and valid. They should also be instructed to guard against doubts and to stand firm in the belief that they have received the Holy Spirit and that the tongues they are speaking are *real*. They should not consider doubting thoughts such as:

That sounds like gibberish!
That's just you, you're just making that up!
You are really going off the "deep end" with all this!
Nothing really happened, you are imaging all this!

Satan will always attempt to reinforce the doubts of the mind. He is a thief and a robber (John 10:10). If he can't keep believers from receiving God's gifts, he will attempt to rob them after they do receive. Believers must be aware of Satan's tactics, stand firm in their faith, believe that they have received the Holy Spirit, and determine not to be robbed by the enemy.

Believers often fear that it is just "them" doing the speaking. The fact is, it is "them"! The Scriptures do not indicate that the Holy Spirit speaks in tongues; we do! The Holy Spirit is poured out on *flesh*! It is our voice that speaks. As long as the mouth is closed, making no effort to speak, the person will not speak in tongues. Psalm 81:10 is appropriate here, "Open your mouth wide, and I will fill it."

Sometimes the initial attempt to speak in tongues is the believer vocalizing natural syllable sounds. As they continue to do this in *faith*, a spiritual language will begin to flow from their spirit. It's similar to priming a pump. As a young girl, I lived on a farm that had an outdoor pump with a long handle. Sometimes the water wouldn't come until we poured water into the top of the pump (priming the pump). After we primed the pump and pumped the handle, the water began to gush out. In the initial attempt to speak in tongues, one may be speaking syllables in the natural (priming the pump—an act of faith) before the spiritual language will flow from our spirit. This is giving corresponding action to our faith.

After believers are baptized in the Holy Spirit, there is a desire and zeal to share their experience. However, they may find that their testimony is not always received so eagerly. Frequently close friends and relatives are the severest critics.

A seminary student in our class was baptized in the Holy Spirit and spoke in tongues fluently. When he related this experience to his instructors, it was not affirmed but ridiculed. Because the response to his testimony was so negative, he soon *doubted* his experience. As a result, he became confused and had difficulty speaking in tongues. When he returned to class, we prayed for him and encouraged him to believe. He left rejoicing in the Lord because he was able to speak in tongues fluently again.

It is good to use wisdom and discernment when we share spiritual experiences. Some may trample on our testimony (Matt. 7:6). We should allow the Holy Spirit to direct us to those to whom we should witness. He knows who will be receptive to our testimony and will cause them to cross our path.

Because baptism in the Holy Spirit is such a wonderful spiritual experience for many believers, there is an eagerness for others to have the same experience. But we must be sensitive and not pressure others to be baptized in the Holy Spirit. The Lord may need to prepare their hearts before they can receive. This was true in my life and Don's. As we look back, we can see how the Lord led us and prepared us. When it was His timing, we were very ready to ask and receive.

In the book of Acts, we read of new converts being baptized in the Holy Spirit at conversion or shortly thereafter, hence it isn't always necessary to have a lengthy time lapse between conversion and baptism in the Holy Spirit. It is the leading of the Holy Spirit that is important.

It is not required that believers have others lay hands on them and pray for them to be baptized in the Holy Spirit, although it certainly is scriptural to do so. In the New Testament church it was common practice. Believers can ask for the Holy Spirit themselves, if they choose to do so and have faith to receive. "For everyone who asks receives" (Luke 11:10). Neither Don nor I had others pray for us. We asked for the Holy Spirit by ourselves and received.

"Baptized in the Spirit" believers need fellowship with like-minded believers. The ideal is to be part of a fellowship of Spirit-filled believers where they can speak of, and experience, the ministry of the Holy Spirit. Sharing our spiritual experiences with others alleviates doubts and misgivings, and "establishes" them in our life.

Believers usually have a heightened sense of the Lord's presence and love after being baptized in the Holy Spirit. As time goes by, this sense and awareness may lessen, causing them to doubt their experience. This may also cause them to fear that they have committed some gross sin or that the Holy Spirit has left them. Not having a consciousness of God's presence does not indicate the Lord isn't with us. The believer's faith must always be based on the Word of God, and in this instance, it is well to remember the following verses of Scripture, "He will never fail us nor forsake us" (Heb. 13:5) and "He is with us always" (Matt. 28:20). Faith is based on what God has said and not on how we feel or what we see! Because it is the Holy Spirit's work to teach the believer to walk the Christian life by faith rather than by feelings or sight, we can expect that there will be times when we do not have a consciousness of His presence.

For we walk by faith, not by sight. 2 Corinthians 5:7

A hindrance to receiving the Holy Spirit is past involvement in the occult or false religions. Things of an occult nature are fortune telling, ouija boards, tarot cards, astrology, witchcraft, and the like. God looks upon these as sin and considers them an abomination (Deut. 18:9-12; Acts 19:18-19). Dabbling in these makes one vulnerable to the snares of Satan. The believer should dispose of occult books or any unholy objects, renounce the occult and false teachings, and confess involvement in these as sin. Scripture declares we are forgiven when we confess our sins (1 John 1:9-10). We may also need to consciously forgive ourselves. There are times, even though we have received God's forgiveness, we continue to berate ourselves for the sins we committed.

Another barrier to receiving baptism in the Holy Spirit is exposure to prejudice about the experience of being baptized in the Holy Spirit. If people have been taught that it is fanaticism, abnormal, or even devilish, it may be difficult for them to have faith to receive. Their minds need to be renewed and enlightened by the Holy Spirit regarding the scriptural truth of this experience.

It is *normal* to have some apprehension when asking to be baptized in the Holy Spirit, because we lack knowledge as to how this will change our life and what the consequences will be. It is moving into an unknown spiritual arena. To counter this fear, we must keep our focus on God, who is a loving Heavenly Father, and trust that He does not give anything harmful or detrimental. He gives good gifts to His children (Matt. 7:11; James 1:17). Jesus said to His disciples that it was to their *advantage* that He go away (John 16:7), because upon His departure, the Holy Spirit would come and He would always be with them (John 14:16). It is to the believer's advantage to be filled with the Holy Spirit.

To be baptized in the Holy Spirit and speak in tongues is not a spiritual status symbol, nor cause for spiritual pride. It is by the grace of God that we receive the gift of the Holy Spirit. Neither does it indicate instant sanctification or spiritual maturity. There is still a need to grow in grace, mature in faith, deny self, take up the cross, put to death the deeds of the flesh, read the Bible, and pray. But the blessing of being baptized in the Holy Spirit will surely *help* us grow spiritually, and come to maturity of faith. It also equips us to be co-laborers with God, who graciously allows us to be part of what He is doing.

Chapter 7

The Gifts of the Holy Spirit

Our God is supernatural and we should expect the supernatural in the body of Christ (church). There are nine Spiritual Gifts of the Holy Spirit (1 Cor. 12:7-11), and they are divinely supernatural. Because baptism in the Holy Spirit is the gateway experience for the Gifts of the Spirit to manifest in the life of the believer, these Gifts usually manifest through Spirit-filled believers. This does not mean that the Gifts cannot operate through any believer; our God is sovereign and can anoint whomever and whenever He chooses. But the Gifts are more apt to manifest through those who have been baptized in the Holy Spirit and speak in tongues, because this experience brings the believer into the power and dimensions of the Spirit that are not realized otherwise. The prophet Joel states that God's people will prophesy when the Spirit is poured out upon them (Joel 2:28).

The Gifts equip the church for ministry. They are manifestations of God's presence and power flowing through believers to edify the church, but may also be a sign to the unbeliever. A manifestation of the divinely supernatural can greatly impress the skeptical unbeliever and cause him to have to deal with the reality of God (1 Cor. 14:24-25).

Scripture reveals that it is the Holy Spirit's mission to glorify Christ and bear witness to Him (John 15:26, 16:14); manifestations of the Gifts of the Spirit are a witness to Christ's resurrection and exaltation. When expressed as the Lord intended, the gifts are glorious and most precious! They are spiritual treasures from God.

Operation of the Spiritual Gifts should be a common occurrence in the church. Paul exhorted the Corinthians to earnestly desire the gifts (1 Cor. 14:1), and not to be ignorant and misinformed about them (1 Cor. 12:1). This also applies to the church today. The Gifts should be considered vital and essential to congregational life, not optional, if the church is to fulfill her appointed destiny. They are also indispensable in preparing God's people for the Second Coming of Christ.

...so that you are not lacking in any spiritual gift, as you wait for the revealing of our Lord Jesus Christ, who will sustain you to the end, guiltless in the day of our Lord Jesus Christ. 1 Corinthians 1:7-8

The Spiritual Gifts are often spoken of as the charismatic gifts of the Holy Spirit. The word "gift" in 1 Corinthians 12 is from the same Greek root as grace—"charis." This indicates that the nine Spiritual Gifts are grace gifts. A definition of grace is "divine enabling," that is, a special endowment by God.

There are three categories of the nine charismatic gifts. The gifts of revelation are Word of Wisdom, Word of Knowledge, and Discerning of Spirits. The gifts of utterance are Prophecy, Various Kinds of Tongues, and Interpretation of Tongues. The power gifts are the Gift of Faith, the Working of Miracles, and the Gifts of Healing. These Spiritual Gifts are listed in 1 Corinthians 12:7-11.

But the manifestation of the Spirit is given to every man to profit withal. For to one is given by the Spirit the word of wisdom; to another the word of knowledge by the same Spirit; to another faith by the same Spirit; to another the gifts of healing by the same Spirit; to another the working of miracles; to another prophecy; to another discerning of spirits; to another divers (various) kinds of tongues; to another the interpretation of tongues. 1 Corinthians 12:7-10 (KJV)

The power and the anointing of the Holy Spirit are essential to prophesy, to work miracles, to heal, to give a word of wisdom from God, to have a word of knowledge that is not learned with the intellect. The power of the Holy Spirit is essential to have the God-kind-of-faith (Mark 11:22), to discern spirits, to speak in various tongues, and to interpret tongues. These Gifts cannot be exercised by a person's natural power. The manifestation gifts of the Holy Spirit are spiritual; they are not natural attributes, nor part of the character of the believer.

The Holy Spirit initiates the Gifts and apportions them to individual believers as He wills. His sovereign will imparts the Gifts of the Spirit.

All these are inspired by one and the same Spirit, who apportions to each one individually as he wills. 1 Corinthians 12:11

As believers are faithful in their calling, the Gifts that are essential to their ministry will manifest through them. It is more important to find our place and ministry in the body of Christ than to be overly concerned about which Gifts will manifest through us. The Gifts are tools for accomplishing the work of the Spirit.

As believers mature spiritually, certain Gifts may operate more frequently and with greater effectiveness through them. This would indicate they have a ministry in those gifts.

A brief overview of the nine Spiritual Gifts of the Holy Spirit follows:

Word of Wisdom: This Gift is a fragment (word) of wisdom imparted supernaturally by the Holy Spirit for a specific situation. It may be directive, indicating a particular action in a situation. The Word of Wisdom often speaks of the future while the Word of Knowledge is usually present or past knowledge.

This Gift is not human wisdom used in dealing with everyday life or application of the wisdom of the world, nor is it theological wisdom obtained from the study of Scripture. It is not general wisdom, but is a portion of divine wisdom that God desires to reveal. Frequently the Word of Wisdom and the Word of Knowledge operate together and may be exercised through the Gift of Prophecy.

In Matthew 17:27, the Lord Jesus had a word of wisdom for Peter when He told him to take the shekel from the mouth of the fish as a tax payment.

Word of Knowledge: This is a word of knowledge imparted supernaturally by the Holy Spirit revealing facts about persons or circumstances for a specific purpose. It is not obtained by studying the Bible or knowing God. Nor is it knowledge gained by the educational process, but it is a fragment (word) of knowledge, supernaturally given by the Holy Spirit for a definite purpose. In Acts 5, Peter received a Word of Knowledge concerning Ananias and Sapphira in their attempt to be deceitful. A Word of Knowledge was given to the Lord Jesus regarding the Samaritan woman at the well (John 4:17-19).

Gift of Faith: This is a portion of God's faith imparted by the Holy Spirit to the believer that enables him to believe for the extraordinary or miraculous. It is a supernatural faith that goes beyond human faith, a faith that speaks of nonexistent things as if they existed (Rom. 4:17). It is not the same as the believer's general faith or saving faith nor is it the fruit of faith. A mustard seed quantity of this divine faith is able to move "mountains" (Matt. 21:21). It is a manifestation of the "God kind" of faith (Mark 11:22).

When the Gift of Faith is in operation, the believer *knows* that what he speaks will come to pass; the result may be immediate or may occur after a period of time. When the Lord Jesus cursed the fig tree, the result wasn't evident until sometime later (Mark 11:14-21). The Gift of Faith receives the miracle, while the Gift of Working of Miracles performs the miracle. Frequently the Gift of Faith and the

Gift of Miracles are merged. Peter was exercising both when he spoke these words to the lame man at the temple gate, "I have no silver or gold, but I give you what I have; in the name of Jesus Christ of Nazareth, walk!" (Acts 3:6).

Gifts of Healing: The Gifts of Healing are given by God to the church to bring healing to people. God desires wholeness for His people, physically, emotionally, and mentally. The results of the Gifts of Healing may be immediate or may occur after a lapse of time. We must not confuse Gifts of Healing with medical science or human knowledge. The Gifts of Healing are supernatural; it is the healing power of God imparted to those in need. Here the word *Gifts* is plural, indicating there are different kinds of healing gifts; one person may have a gift of healing for a particular disease and others may have healing gifts for other illnesses. In charismatic Christian circles we may hear the terms *inner healing* or *healing of memories*. These terms refer to the healing of emotional and psychological traumas resulting from abuse, neglect, and rejection. Many in the body of Christ have wounded spirits and broken hearts that need this type of healing. The Lord Jesus said that He came to save the crushed in spirit and heal the brokenhearted (Isa. 61:1, Psalm 34:18). Psalm 23 states that the Lord restores our soul.

He heals the brokenhearted, and binds up their wounds. Psalm 147:3

But by sorrow of the heart the spirit is broken. Proverbs 15:13b (KJV)

Gift of Working of Miracles: This gift is the manifestation of God's supernatural power through human instruments, called Working of Miracles. It is usually an immediate event, altering the normal course of nature. God may do *creative* miracles such as growth of a leg where there was none, or straightening of a deformed limb. In operation, the Gift of Miracles is the omnipotent, supernatural, magnificent power of God manifesting to meet a need. Miracles truly glorify God and often operate in the ministry of the evangelist, thus confirming the gospel that is proclaimed to the unsaved.

Gift of Prophecy: In the manifestation of this Gift, the believer becomes a spokesperson speaking God's message in the vernacular. Simple prophecy, which all believers may exercise, is primarily for exhortation, comfort, encouragement, and edification. All may prophesy, but not all will be called to the office of a prophet. The prophetic utterances of a prophet may be of a revelatory nature and may include words of reproof, exposure of sin, and warnings of judgment.

Scripture states that our knowledge is imperfect and our prophecy is imperfect (1 Cor. 13:9). Prophecies (New Testament era) are a product of God and the believer; there is a human element involved in the prophetic utterances, a merging of the human and the divine in its manifestation. This is why it is important for those who exercise the Gift of Prophecy to have instruction and oversight. The leadership of a church should provide instruction, pastoral oversight, and opportunities for members to prophesy in order for them to grow and mature in the exercise of this Gift. This equips the saints for ministry (Eph. 4:12). If there is no occasion for them to prophesy, they will be hindered in learning how to exercise the Gift properly, resulting in its misuse. When there is abuse and misuse of the Gift of Prophecy, it will ultimately be despised and as a result, the Spirit will be quenched (1 Thess. 5:19-20), and eventually all prophesying will cease. Thus the body of Christ will suffer loss, for the Gift of Prophecy edifies the community of faith. The emotion of God is usually evident in prophecy; this is not apparent in other ministries, such as preaching and teaching. Prophetic utterances that convey and express the emotion of God, albeit through inadequate human channels, bring great joy, blessing, and enthusiasm to the saints. Prophecy appeals more to the emotions while teaching appeals to the intellect.

When someone in great need receives a prophetic word, which expresses God's emotion of love, it can be of enormous benefit and comfort, and also strengthening of faith. Paul encouraged the Corinthian believers to prophesy (1 Cor. 14:5, 31).

The Gift of Prophecy is not the delivery of a prepared sermon. Preaching is proclaiming and explaining what one already knows, and requires preparation. Prophecy is proclaiming the mind of God by the inspiration and prompting of the Holy Spirit. One does not prepare a prophecy. However, the Gift of Prophecy may manifest during the preaching of a sermon, but it is not the same as preaching. Scripture indicates that people are saved, not through prophecy, but through preaching (1 Cor. 1:21). Prophecies given in assemblies need to be judged and evaluated as to whether they are in agreement with Scripture. True prophecies are never contrary to Scripture, neither should they be harsh or condemnatory. Believers should be discerning when they receive a directive prophecy; a prophetic word of this nature should be confirmed before acting on it. Revelation 19:10 proclaims that the testimony of Jesus is the spirit of prophecy.

Discerning of Spirits: This is divine ability given by the Holy Spirit that enables the believer to discern the spiritual realm and distinguish between the Spirit of God, angels, the human spirit, and the spirits of Satan. It is not primarily discerning Satan's realm. When this gift is operating, the believer can discern whether it is the Holy Spirit, the human spirit, or an evil spirit that is prompting a particular action. Paul was exercising the Gift of Discerning of Spirits when he identified the spirit of divination in the young woman at Philippi (Acts 16:16-18).

This is a valuable gift when ministering to those who need deliverance from the demonic. Since evil spirits can cause diseases and illnesses, through the exercise of this Gift, they can be identified and people can be delivered and be healed of diseases. In Luke 13:10-16, Jesus discerned a spirit of infirmity in the woman who was bent over. He set her free and she was healed. Believers who are involved in the occult before they are saved may need deliverance from demonic spirits and, in these situations, this Gift is essential. At times, this Gift may be merged with the Gifts of Healing.

A person who has the Gift of Discerning of Spirits frequently receives visions and is able to *see* into the spiritual realm as God permits. This Gift is in operation when people experience angel visitations. Many times both in the Old and New Testament, the people of God received guidance, encouragement, and strength from the appearance of angels.

This Gift was also apparent on the Mount of Transfiguration when Peter, James, and John were permitted to behold the glorified Christ and see Moses and Elijah speaking with the Lord. There are many examples in the Bible of the Gift of Discerning of Spirits. In the Old Testament Elisha sees the chariot and horses of fire as they separated him from Elijah as he was taken up (2 Kings 2:11-12).

Various Kinds of Tongues: The Gift of Various Kinds of Tongues is a message spoken in tongues, usually a public utterance, which requires interpretation. In the manifestation of this Gift, a believer is prompted by the Spirit to speak aloud in tongues in an assembly of believers. This is followed with the manifestation of the Gift of Interpretation. It is a word from God to His people, similar to the Gift of Prophecy. One difference is that the supernatural aspect of speaking in tongues causes a congregation to become alert and attentive to the word that the Holy Spirit will give in the exercise of the Gift of Interpretation of Tongues.

The manifestation of the Gift of Tongues may also be prayer. By the Spirit, God prompts someone to offer a prayer in tongues. God answers this prayer in the manifestation of the Gift of Prophecy. This can account for the difference in length between the tongues spoken and the interpretation.

Interpretation of Tongues: This Gift is given by the Holy Spirit to interpret a message given in tongues. It may be a perfect translation but usually is not. The Gift is Interpretation of Tongues, not translation of tongues. The interpretation may provide a general sense of what has been said, with different phrasing. This may be why, on occasion, there is a difference in length between the message and the interpretation. The one who gives the message in tongues may also exercise the Gift of Interpretation. The apostle Paul encouraged those who gave utterances in tongues to pray for the power to interpret.

The Spiritual Gifts operate in partnership with God. Indeed they are of God, but the operation of them also depends on the believers. Exercising the Gifts is a cooperation between God and the believer. The merging of the human and divine is true of all the Gifts of the Spirit. The believer is required to obey the prompting of the Holy Spirit and move in boldness of faith exercising the Gift. Believers bear responsibility for the proper exercise of the Gifts. If the manifestations of the Gifts of the Spirit were entirely the sovereign work of the Spirit, the Gifts would always be exercised perfectly. The believer has free will in the operation of the Gifts; there is no compulsion in their exercise. It is a learning process for the believer to exercise the Gifts of the Spirit properly. Misuse and abuse of the Gifts is usually due to fear, carnality, or ignorance. Mistakes will be made, but God is patient and ever present to help and teach us. Because God is patient with us, believers should also be patient with one another as they learn to move in the Gifts of the Spirit. Everyone begins as a novice. Practice and courage to move in faith are necessary. It is important for believers to be under spiritually mature shepherding as they exercise the Gifts.

When operating in the Gifts, one should guard against spiritual pride; manifesting Spiritual Gifts does not indicate spiritual maturity. The Corinthian church did not lack in any gift (1 Cor. 1:7), yet the apostle Paul indicated they were still "men of the flesh" (1 Cor. 3:1-3) and required correction.

When the Gifts of the Holy Spirit are exercised, they are *often blended and do not always operate independently.* It may be difficult to determine where one gift begins and the other ends; the boundaries are not always well defined. Frequently a Word of Knowledge or a Word of Wisdom is given through the Gift of Prophecy. Discerning of Spirits and Gifts of Healing are often merged. When Jesus raised Lazarus from the dead, He spoke the words, "Lazarus, come forth." At that time the Gift of Faith, the Gift of Miracles, and the Gift of Healing were exercised (John 11). This merging of Gifts is of minor importance since the Holy Spirit inspires them all.

It has been said that Christians should seek the "Giver" and not the Gifts. This appears spiritual and pious but is not scriptural. Of course, we are to seek the Lord above all else, but Scripture does admonish God's people to "earnestly desire" the Gifts (1 Cor. 14:1). Desiring the Gifts and allowing them to be exercised through us with the right motive *is* seeking the Lord and walking in obedience to Him. To truly desire fellowship with God is to desire the supernatural realm of the Spirit, because God is supernatural. We were created for fellowship in the Spirit (2 Cor. 13:14).

Some believe it is more spiritual to have love rather than seek the Gifts. It is important to distinguish between the two. Love is a fruit of the Spirit (Gal. 5:22-23). It is to become part of our character and is a growth process; the Gifts of the Spirit are not part of us, they manifest through us as the Holy Spirit initiates. Love is the framework in which the Gifts operate. We naturally desire to give gifts to those we love. We may love someone who is ill, but that alone will not heal. How wonderful it is when Gifts of Healing manifest for those we love and they are healed! When the needs of the people are met by the operation of the Gifts of the Holy Spirit, *it is the love of Christ* being ministered through God's people. It's not love or gifts, but rather love plus the gifts of the Holy Spirit. They both come from the Holy Spirit and should supplement one another; they are not in competition. The fruit of the Spirit exhibits character. The Gifts of the Spirit exhibit ability.

God places great value and emphasis on Christlike character (1 Corinthians 13), but having Christlike character does not eliminate the need for the Gifts of the Holy Spirit. The Lord Jesus is the epitome of love, and the Gifts of the Spirit operated freely and perfectly through Him during His earthly ministry.

The apostle Paul does not say that the manifestations of the Spirit without love are not genuine. The person exercising the Gift without love has the imperfection. Even without love, the Gifts may still be of value to the church but the *person* is nothing and *he* gains nothing without love (1 Cor. 13:2).

If I speak in the tongues of men and of angels, but have not love, I am a noisy gong or a clanging cymbal. And if I have prophetic powers, and understand all mysteries and all knowledge, and if I have all faith, so as to remove mountains, but have not love, I am nothing. If I give away all I have, and if I deliver my body to be burned, but have not love, I gain nothing.
1 Corinthians 13:1-3

In 1 Corinthians 13, Paul defines love to the Corinthian church; cultivating this fruit of the Spirit would be an antidote to the carnality that was prevalent in that church. He exhorts them to grow in love and fervently desire spiritual endowments.

Love is patient and kind; love is not jealous or boastful; it is not arrogant or rude. Love does not insist on its own way; it is not irritable or resentful; it does not rejoice at wrong, but

93

rejoices in the right. Love bears all things, believes all things, hopes all things, endures all things. 1 Corinthians 13:4-7

Make love your aim, and earnestly desire the spiritual gifts, especially that you may prophesy. 1 Corinthians 14:1

Churches should strive for the Gifts to manifest in their community of faith, and not be indifferent, fearful, and unbelieving concerning them. Allowing the Holy Spirit to be *sovereign* in the life of the church will build up and edify the church, causing believers to grow in the fruit of the Spirit, which is primarily love. If we have the fruit of love, other spiritual fruit will develop also.

But the fruit of the Spirit is love, joy, peace, patience, kindness, goodness, faithfulness, gentleness, self-control; against such there is no law. Galatians 5:22-23

The Gifts of the Holy Spirit will operate properly when motivated by a desire to bless and help others. God has placed them in the church so that she, the church, might truly be a witness and testimony to the risen Lord Jesus Christ. Our God is a God of *power* and *love*; both of these attributes of God should be seen in the church. Paul admonishes the church to be *aglow* with the Spirit and to serve the Lord.

Never flag in zeal, be aglow with the Spirit, serve the Lord. Romans 12:11

All glory and praise to the Lord!

Selected Bibliography

The Full Life Study Bible, KJV New Testament. Grand Rapids, Mich.: Life Publishers International, 1990.

Gee, Donald. *Concerning Spiritual Gifts*. Springfield, Mo.: Radiant Books, Revised 1972, 1980.

Green, Jay P., Jr., ed. *Pocket Interlinear New Testament*. Grand Rapids, Mich.: Baker Book House, 1979, 1980.

Hagin, Kenneth E. *Concerning Spiritual Gifts*. Tulsa, Okla.: Faith Library Publications, 1986.

Harper, Michael. *Spiritual Warfare*. Plainfield, N.J.: Logos International, 1970.

The Layman's Commentary on the Holy Spirit. Plainfield, N.J.: Logos International, 1972.

Lea, Larry. *The Hearing Ear*. Altamonte Springs, Fla.: Creation House, Strang Communications Co., 1988.

Lindsay, Gordon. *Gifts of the Holy Spirit, Volumes 1-4*. Dallas: Christ for the Nations, Reprinted 1983, 1986, 1989.

Nee, Watchman. *The Release of the Spirit*. Cloverdale, Ind.: Sure Foundation Publishers, 1965.

Nee, Watchman. *The Spiritual Man*. New York: Christian Fellowship Publishers, 1968.

Nee, Watchman. *The Testimony of God*. New York: Christian Fellowship Publishers, 1979.

Prince, Derek. *The Spirit Filled Believer's Handbook*. Altamonte Springs, Fla.: Creation House, Strang Communications Co., 1993.

Torrey, R. A. *The Person & Work of the Holy Spirit*. Grand Rapids, Mich.: Zondervan Publishing House, 1910.

Wallis, Arthur. *The Radical Christian*. Old Tappan, N.J.: Fleming N. Revell Company, 1981.

ORDER FORM

To order additional copies of **You Shall Be Baptized In The Holy Spirit,** complete the information below.

Ship to: (Please print)
Name   _____

Address   _____

City, State, Zip   _____

Day Phone   _____

_____Copie(s) of above book @$6.95 each $_____

Packing and shipping $_____
   ($1.60 for the first book, $0.50 for each
   additional book. Will be shipped book rate.)
Minnesota residents add 6.5% tax $_____

Total Amount enclosed $_____

Make checks payable to Eldo Publishers

**Send to: Eldo Publishers
2074 Pleasantview Drive
New Brighton, MN 55112**